TRAVEL BY TRAIN

Michael E. Zega and John E. Gruber

TRAVEL BY TRAIN

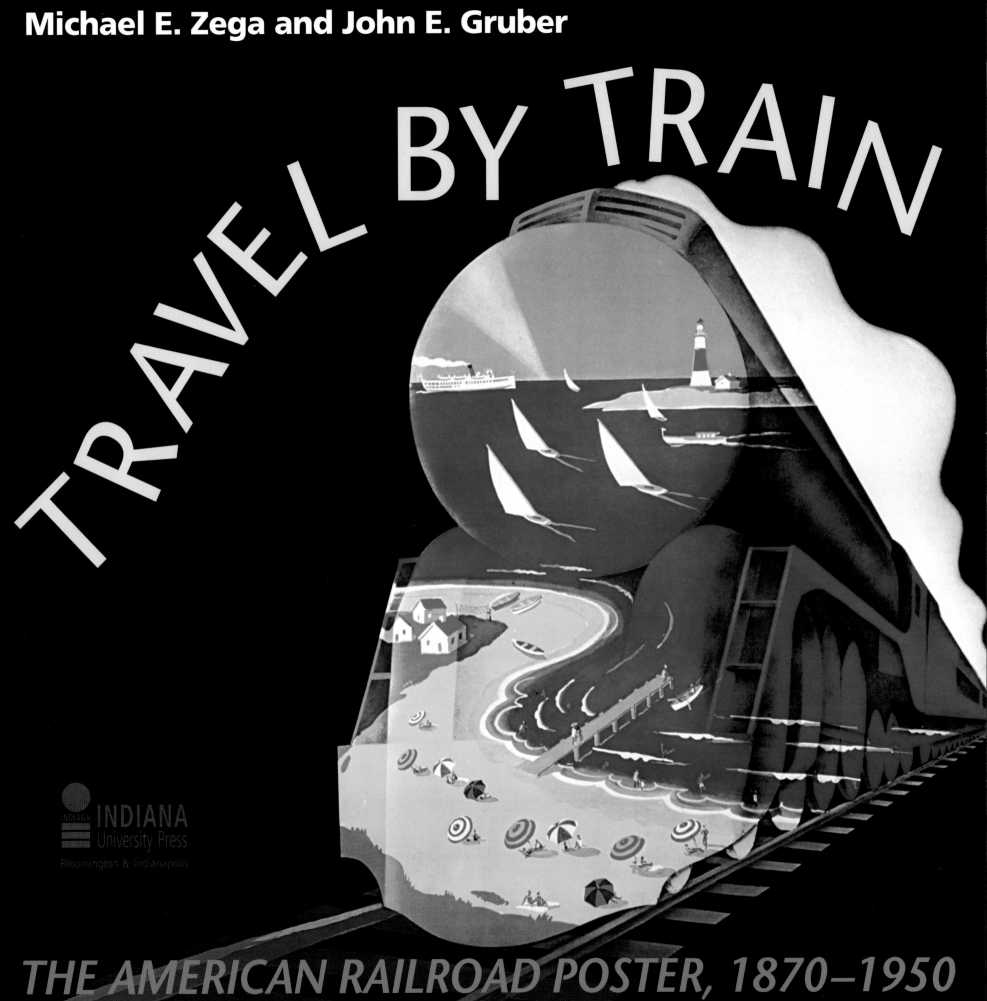

INDIANA
University Press
Bloomington & Indianapolis

THE AMERICAN RAILROAD POSTER, 1870–1950

This book is a publication of

Indiana University Press
601 North Morton Street
Bloomington, Indiana 47404-3797 USA

http://iupress.indiana.edu

Telephone orders   800-842-6796
Fax orders   812-855-7931
Orders by e-mail   iuporder@indiana.edu

The paper used in this publication meets the minimum requirements of American
National Standard for Information Sciences—Permanence of Paper for Printed
Library Materials, ANSI Z39.48-1984.

Printed in China

Library of Congress Cataloging-in-Publication Data

Zega, Michael E., date
  Travel by train : the American railroad poster, 1870–1950 / Michael E.
Zega and John E. Gruber.
       p.   cm.
Includes bibliographical references and index.
  ISBN 0-253-34152-3 (alk. paper)
  1. Railroads—Posters.   2. Posters, American—19th century.
3. Posters, American—20th century.   I. Gruber, John E., date   II. Title.
  NC1849.R34 Z44 2002
  741.6'74'0973—dc21
                          2002002516

1   2   3   4   5   07   06   05   04   03   02

CONTENTS

Preface | vii

Acknowledgments | ix

Introduction | xi

ONE. **Before 1900**

Early Poster Antecedents | 1

The Rise of Competition | 2

The Lure of Place | 6

1890s: "Reason Why" Advertising | 9

The Lithographed Display Poster | 10

Oscar Binner's Gigantic Images | 17

TWO. **1900–1909**

Advertising Revolution | 21

1900: Urban Display Windows | 23

Design in the New Century | 30

Car Cards | 30

THREE. **The Teens**

Emerging Corporate Imagery | 38

The Power of Symbol: Louis Treviso's Santa Fe Posters | 39

FOUR. **The 1920s**

Railroad Advertising Transformed | 48

Santa Fe and Sam Hyde Harris | 50

Southern Pacific and Maurice Logan | 52

Back East: The New Haven Begins | 63

New York Central's Art Posters | 63

Hernando G. Villa and the Santa Fe *Chief* | 74

The Canadian Pacific and Others | 81

FIVE. **The 1930s**

Depression-Era Innovation | 93

Leslie Ragan | 94

Snow Trains | 97

The Streamliner Image | 103

The Southern Pacific Studio | 109

Sascha Maurer: The Appeal of the Machine | 111

Ragan's Streamliners | 124

POSTSCRIPT | 125

Bibliography | 133

Index | 137

PREFACE

There are no ready-made resources for information about American railroad travel posters. Advertising sources barely mention the railroads and their pioneering promotional efforts. The artists seldom are identified, and, if they are, they are difficult to find in the standard biographical indexes. For most, archives do not exist.

So, of necessity, this book has relied heavily on contemporary advertising journals, listed in the bibliography. Michael Zega uncovered the information by painstakingly reading dozens of the periodicals. No indexes are available, and some of the significant items are not even cited in the tables of contents. Without the extensive resources of the New York Public Library, the research would have been much more difficult.

The results have been rewarding. A treasure trove of information has been uncovered about the posters and their place in the railroad and general advertising practices of the time. From this emerges, for the first time, a comprehensive understanding of the posters' value as an advertising tool for the railroad companies, plus identification of the poster artists themselves. The companies, in turn, receive recognition of their rightful place in the development of modern advertising—a role ignored in many advertising histories.

You will find a full review of posters from coast to coast. Credit for creative posters often goes to the eastern railroads, such as the New York Central and New Haven lines. Certainly they produced outstanding posters. But we have found, in preparing this book, that the seldom-mentioned Southern Pacific was the most prolific, and the Santa Fe offered consistent quality and innovation over a long period of time. And who would expect regional lines such as the Monon and Chicago Great Western to have an important role in the story?

The text and images concentrate on the main line railroads. Thus Samuel Insull's rapid transit and electric interurban lines in the Chicago area, as well as the Oakland Antioch & Eastern/Sacramento Northern in California, are not included.

The book had its beginnings in a series of *Vintage Rails* magazine articles, followed by articles in *Classic Trains*. This collection of posters brings new insights about North American travel and advertising practice. We hope you enjoy reading it as much as we have enjoyed producing it.

Acknowledgments

The authors wish to acknowledge the assistance of their many contributors. Nicholas Lowry, president of Swann Galleries in New York City, provided an invaluable resource in tracking down hard-to-find images. Helga Maurer Wagner and Marilyn Hinners shared family photos and recollections about artists Sascha Maurer and Leslie Ragan, both of whom loom large in the story. Two contemporary railroads also made substantial contributions. Union Pacific's Don Snoddy and Bill Kratville tracked down and copied many an obscure image. At the Burlington Northern Santa Fe, curator Suzanne Burris proved invaluable in answering questions and providing access to the historic AT&SF art collection.

Thanks to individual contributors: Arthur Dubin, Charles Stats, Hugh T. Guillaume, Judi Leavelle, Maurine St. Gaudens, Tracy Logan Immordino, Nancy Boas, Edan M. Hughes, Virginia Couse Leavitt, and Paul Sichert. Finally, artist Paul Carey's capable recollection provided a look back in time to peers Louis Treviso and Maurice Logan.

And to institutions: The Huntington Library's Alan Jutzi; Ellen Halteman of the California State Railroad Museum Library; Kim Walters, librarian of the Southwest Museum, Los Angeles; Connie Menninger of the Kansas State Historical Society, Topeka; Jessica Meyer at the Chicago Historical Society; Ellen Gartrell and Jacquelyn Reid of Duke University Library; Kurt Bell of the Railroad Museum of Pennsylvania; Chuck Blardone, editor of the PRRT&HS journal, *The Keystone;* Terry Brown of The Society of Illustrators, New York City; Diana Dayton and Dorothy King of East Hampton Library; Beth Diefendorf of the New York Public Library; Kay Bost of DeGolyer Library, Southern Methodist University; Sarah Bennett of the Albany Institute of History and Art; and Silvia Ros at the Wolfsonian Foundation, Miami Beach.

Commercial: Joern Weigelt of PosterConnection, Inc., San Mateo, California; Jack Rennert of Posters Please, Inc., New York City; and George Theofiles of Miscellaneous Man, New Freedom, Pennsylvania.

Photography by Jean Pierre Bonin; map design by Colby Waller.

The book project started in the hands of Thomas H. Garver, Madison, Wisconsin, but he soon handed it over to us. We thank him for his confidence in us.

Poster Resources

Swann Galleries at 104 East 25th Street, New York, NY 10010-2977, auctions vintage posters and specializes in American railroad examples.

Posters Please, Inc., 601 West 26th Street, New York, NY 10001, auctions vintage posters, as does PosterConnection, 3921 Pasadena Drive, Suite 300, San Mateo, CA 94403.

Publication of this book is made possible in part with the assistance of a Challenge Grant from the National Endowment for the Humanities, a federal agency that supports research, education, and public programming in the humanities; and with the generous support of the Friends of Indiana University Press.

INTRODUCTION

Writing during the 1930s, artist Sascha Maurer suggested that designing travel posters was likely the greatest ambition of every young commercial artist. Experience allowed him the insight that the endeavor offered wide creative range, but in return demanded a great deal of imagination. In practice, the travel poster proved an elusive medium that few artists mastered. Maurer's work for the New Haven Railroad placed him among that select group. He characterized the poster as a speed medium, where first impressions were everything. "Few colors, vivid, attention-compelling; striking, well-disposed composition; short and smashing copy." These, he argued, "are the attributes that make a poster successful."

If ever there existed a match of medium and subject, it was surely that of the display poster and railroad travel. The poster's vivid color effects and focused, instantaneous message were perfectly suited to promoting the romance of the rails—the lure of faraway places, dramatic mountain vistas, the peaceful hush of a sleeper berth speeding through the night. For more than a century, the railroad dominated American travel, opening the West, revolutionizing personal mobility, engendering controversy, myth, and romantic lore. Railroad men well understood their subject's dramatic potential and promoted their services accordingly: They virtually invented the illustrated booklet, pioneered in using the halftone, and produced countless timetables, calendars, and posters.

From the first broadsides of the 1830s, American railroad posters evolved in an idiosyncratic manner. Although American advertisers never quite embraced the poster medium with the Europeans' enthusiasm, a few intrepid railroad men provided the fortunate exception. In the competitive tumult of the American economy, firms typically sought readily recognizable, brightly colored designs and reinforced them with prominent headlines and sales claims. American railroad posters most often depicted scenic vistas and speeding locomotives, as did their better-known European counterparts, but there the similarity ended.

The best American work combined the national taste for realistic illustration with vivid color effects and subjects of unusual interest to create images of compelling intensity. Elegant women paused to reflect, limiteds soared across the sky, butlers waited in attendance, Native Americans performed ancient rituals, and streamliners raced through shimmering landscapes. Although neglected for decades as the railroads declined, a remarkable body of work survives to document an adventurous, imaginative era.

This book describes the development of the American railroad poster over the period of its greatest utility, 1870 to 1950. It presents the most important and successful examples and discusses the men and competitive conditions that prompted their production. It reviews about 160 poster images showing spectacular scenery, feature trains, terminals, and special events. Poster dimensions that deviate from the standard single sheet are noted in the captions.

It also provides biographical details about the artists and railroaders who produced the posters, and if available, their life dates. However, for some names, even brief biographies were difficult to find. For many artists, this book offers the first recognition of their contributions to our heritage. All in all, the book presents a comprehensive understanding of the railroad industry's role in promoting artists and their works.

TTTTTTTTTTTT

TRAVEL BY TRAIN

ONE Before 1900

It thus will be seen that advertising plays a powerful part in the drama of the railway; that the railway uses advertising as a sword's point with which to best its rivals.

—*Printers' Ink,* 1892[1]

Early Poster Antecedents

The poster was among the first advertising media, gaining popularity because it provided images in an era before the advent of newspaper illustration. From the early years of the nineteenth century, American firms had used handbills, circulars, and broadsides—tall, rectangular sheets dominated by large type—to promote their goods. Historian James Norris explains that the objective of early advertising was to provide consumers with essential information: the availability, cost, and characteristics of products. Early railroad circulars and broadsides served the same function.[2]

The railroad poster evolved from two disparate sources. First was the uniquely American tradition of circus and show posters, a rough-and-tumble billboard heritage that only began to receive artistic consideration in the early 1890s. Second was that of the decorative art poster, introduced in France by Jules Chèret in 1867. Indeed, early advertising leader Frank Presbrey and art historian Alain Weill both argue that Americans pioneered the large poster and developed the lithographic color poster. Initially printed from woodcuts, by the early 1880s posters were increasingly produced by means of lithography, the process by which the artist or draftsman drew directly on a lithographic stone, the direct medium of transference to the poster sheet. This change also fostered consistency of size: Stones generally measured 30 by 40 inches, thereby creating a standard dimension and designation, the "single sheet" poster.[3]

The railroad poster's roots trace back to the construction of the nation's first railroads in the 1830s. As soon as the new lines stretched but ten or twenty miles, posted signs and broadsides appeared, bearing bold-type announcements of destinations, schedules, equipment, and fares. As time passed, railroad men began to illustrate their broadsides with simple drawings of locomotives and trains.

Many early railroad works were designed and printed by lithographers who produced circus and show posters, and reflected their characteristically colorful, unsophisticated style. The railroad poster, like the circus poster, brimmed with a vast amount of information, and used an array of bright colors. According to lithographer Nelson Strobridge they followed the idea then in vogue "that a presentation of all the features . . . was the most effective form of advertising."[4] It was natural that the railroad poster artists adopted the showmen's style. The advent of the railroad facilitated the touring companies' business and produced a synergistic effect.

The best early productions graphically communicated the import of the new transportation mode. "The Great American Lake Shore Railroads" of 1855–56 clearly incorporated the circus poster's theatricality. Its designers framed the lines' inaugural announcement with a proscenium arch and red-and-blue striped drapery. Its triumphal arch communicated stability and prosperity, while striking colors added a patriotic note (fig. 1). Union Pacific's well-known announcement of the May 1869 opening of the first transcontinental railroad provides another classic example. Printed in four colors, it managed to incorporate a dozen separate headlines and pictured an elk standing astride the West's virgin forests and plains (fig. 2).

As traffic increased during the 1870s, railroad men began to augment posters with a broad range of media. They placed standing timetable advertisements in on-line newspapers to provide ready consumer reference. They also began to advertise with the objective of generating new business, introducing the often-disingenuous "reading notice" format, a block of text run in newspapers and magazines and designed to blend with, and be interpreted as, editorial copy. The era also marked the advent of booklet advertising, a second illustrated format of which railroaders in particular made extensive use. As a result, the poster's function became more specialized. Most now announced special events: mass movements, especially excursions to religious conventions and veterans' reunions. A similar variant was the immigration broadside, production of which boomed during the 1880s as U.S. immigration soared.

The Rise of Competition

Modern advertising would not have been possible if the railroads had not spread like arteries into every section of America, transforming deserts and prairies into towns and cities, creating a single market out of ten thousand isolations.

—1929 Westvaco ad

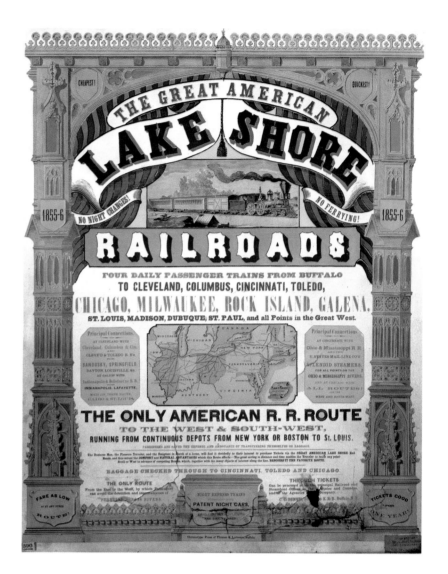

Fig. 1. (ABOVE) Lake Shore Railroads, 1855–56, 27⅝" x 22⅛". Albany Institute of History & Art.

Fig. 2. (FACING PAGE) Union Pacific broadside, May 10, 1869, 8½" x 20⅞". Union Pacific Historical Collection. #501950.

The dynamic of railroad competition that emerged during the 1880s set railroad advertising patterns and largely determined the development of the American railroad poster. During the 1880s railroad construction reached a fever pitch as the complementary regional systems that had developed the nation's railroad network built into one another's territory. This wholesale expansion introduced the phenomenon of multiple competing lines between important business centers and abruptly changed the way railroads did business.

The expanding railroad network also allowed widespread distribution for the first time, creating a national market, and the economies of scale necessary for effective advertising. That the advertising industry developed in tandem with the nation's railroads is evidenced in a remarkable confluence of events: Philadelphian Frederick Ives invented the halftone process—the first means of reproducing an image on a printed page without the interpretive interference of the human hand—in February 1881, just six months before the Pennsylvania Railroad introduced the "limited" train, which rolled west from the very same city.[5] The halftone sparked a boom in illustrated advertising media, particularly national-circulation magazines, which quickly ended the poster's dominance. The limited owed its birth to the rise of competition, the force that would shape railroad advertising for the next seventy-five years.

Throughout the 1880s and well into the 1890s competing companies vied to offer the traveling public the greatest comfort and convenience for their money. Their competitive rivalries were based on a uniquely skewed hypothesis. Although freight traffic produced their chief source of revenue, American railroads targeted their advertising at passengers, on the axiom that "a man 'ships' his merchandise by the route he travels." Thus, promoting passenger traffic was viewed as a means to the more important end of securing an increase in freight.[6]

Railroad advertising invariably focused on two topics: traffic between competitive points and the development of virgin territory, most often the settlement of the West. By the beginning of the twentieth century, competition had grown so intense that the leading trains and even entire passenger departments were often characterized as advertisements.[7]

As the 1880s began, railroad leaders grappled with competition's effects by seeking to establish competitive advantage and build brand identity. Developments in poster and large-format advertising reflected that process.

In response to the new pressures, railroads increasingly made use of unsubstantiated and exaggerated advertising claims. At a time when advertisements routinely strained credibility and employed deception, the railroads were no laggards. Most pervasive was the superlative; each became the "best line," the "most popular route," maker of the "lowest rate." One prominent railroader quipped that every line boasted a map that showed it to be the shortest and most direct to every important point in the United States. South Pacific Coast Railway's (a Southern

Pacific subsidiary) "Switzerland of America" promised the impossible: "No Dust, No Mosquitos, Short Line, Heavy Rail"—characteristic of the era's exaggeration (fig. 3).

The era's seemingly endless parade of technological innovations—dining cars, vestibules, higher speeds—prompted a second frequently used competitive strategy. The railroaders now sought to best one another with the sales appeal of innovation and comfort. As long as the improvements continued apace this approach proved an easy and most effective strategy. Typical was an 1877 steel-plate engraving produced for the Chicago, Burlington & Quincy, one of the first lines to operate dining cars. It depicted an elaborate dinner service, while its copy employed the ephemeral claim of exclusivity (fig. 4).

The new competition further demanded that consumers be made aware of their choices in planning a trip and selecting a carrier. Competition thus spurred the need to gain consumer recognition by establishing a brand identity. Communicating exactly where each line went now became a prime objective. The wall maps, calendars, and posters of the 1880s demonstrate this emphasis. Indeed, for as long as railroads carried passengers, a substantial amount of their energy went into maintaining their individual shares in competitive markets.

Distinctive railroad trademarks, or symbols, first appeared in the early 1880s. Their advent marked the beginning of the railroads' attempts at building brand recognition. Daniel M. Lord, president of the pioneering Chicago advertising agency Lord & Thomas, claimed to have introduced the first trademark in 1881, for the Burlington Route (Chicago, Burlington & Quincy).[8] The Burlington's distinctive rectangle—first printed in black, then in red—spawned the parallelogram-shaped symbols of its two Midwest rivals, the Chicago, Milwaukee & St. Paul and the Chicago & North Western.

Later and most famously, the Pennsylvania Railroad adopted its keystone, in recognition of its namesake state. The PRR keystone dominated an elegant 1883 broadside promoting the line's *New York & Chicago Limited*, so named for its limited number of cars and stops. The association evidently worked, as within a few years the train was popularly known as the *Pennsylvania Limited* (fig. 5). Not to be outdone, the Baltimore & Ohio, another prime competitor for East Coast–Midwest traffic, appropriated perhaps the most effective trademark of them all by picturing the U.S. capitol dome over the copyline "All Trains run via Washington" (fig. 6).

Within a decade, nearly every line had taken to displaying its "logo" (so named after the typeset version) on ads, timetables, and freight cars. In an 1890 address about advertising practice Edward O. McCormick (1858–1923), then general passenger agent (GPA) of the Big Four system, exhorted his peers: "Have a trade mark and use it. Use it everywhere. . . . put it on your freight cars and plaster it wherever you can. People will unconsciously learn it, and will recognize it wherever it may be."[9]

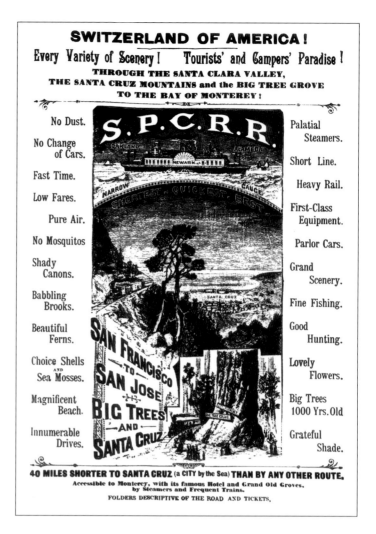

Fig. 3. (FACING PAGE TOP) South Pacific Coast Railway, ca. 1880. Union Pacific Historical Collection.

Fig. 4. (FACING PAGE BOTTOM) Chicago, Burlington & Quincy steel engraving, 1877, 18" x 23".

Fig. 5. (LEFT) Pennsylvania Railroad broadside, 1883, 16" x 33". Chicago Historical Society.

Fig. 6. (ABOVE) Baltimore & Ohio logo, ca. 1890.

More than most, E. O. McCormick evidenced an inclination to experiment with innovative advertising displays. Throughout the decade and for a succession of employers he produced an array of advertising with the objective of communicating exactly where his line went, information that gained in importance as parallel lines multiplied. The Rock Island was the first line to address the problem, in a series of illustrated ads ca. 1881, which showed a traveling salesman examining a large railroad map: "A Man who is unacquainted with the geography of the country, will see by examining this map that the Chicago, Rock Island & Pacific is the Great Connecting Link between East & West!" read the copyline. Many lines imitated this approach, but McCormick's solution gained the most attention. He took the map concept a step further, adding bold color and graphics. His 1887 Monon Route poster featured the eye-catching image of an alligator designed to symbolize the line's Pullman service to Florida and the Deep South (fig. 7).

Still, it was James J. Charlton, GPA of the Chicago & Alton, who most effectively addressed the problem. He selected as his medium an illustrated wall calendar, a choice that also afforded the advantage of ongoing reference and utility. His display innovation marked the second important step in the process of branding railroad service. Produced in colors, Charlton's design featured a standing female figure draped in a long gown designed to outline his line's terminals. Chicago appeared near her head, St. Louis at her feet, and Kansas City on the gown's trailing edge. To better gain attention, he chose for his model Lillie Langtry, the most famously beautiful woman of her day; admirers quickly dubbed her the "Alton Girl" (fig. 8).[10]

Charlton's initiative spurred countless imitations. In 1885 the Big Four Route introduced its calendar, topped by a huge red "4," meant to symbolize the four prominent cities that the line linked together.[11] In 1891 the Wabash, which promoted itself as "the Banner Route," employed a multiple-page calendar that featured the flags of the states it served. In 1897 the St. Paul began producing its own line of calendar beauties. By 1899 the calendars were pervasive: Chicago Great Western offered F. A. Rinehart's colorized photos of Indian chiefs; the Lehigh Valley, a steel engraving of its *Black Diamond Express;* the Santa Fe, artist E. A. Burbank's famed Indian portraits. "The Alton Art Calendar," as Charlton dubbed it, grew famous for introducing a new "Alton Girl" each year; the "fencing girl," "'cow-boy' girl," and "gypsy girl" were popular. By the turn of the century, Charlton had brought about a national calendar craze.

The Lure of Place

If the packed theatre houses of the Bowery presented so many of those gallop-and-shoot "horse operas," the reason is that America was experiencing a fascination with the West. Beyond the setting sun lay the gold of Nevada and California. Beyond the setting sun lay the cedar-felling ax, the buffalo's huge Babylonian

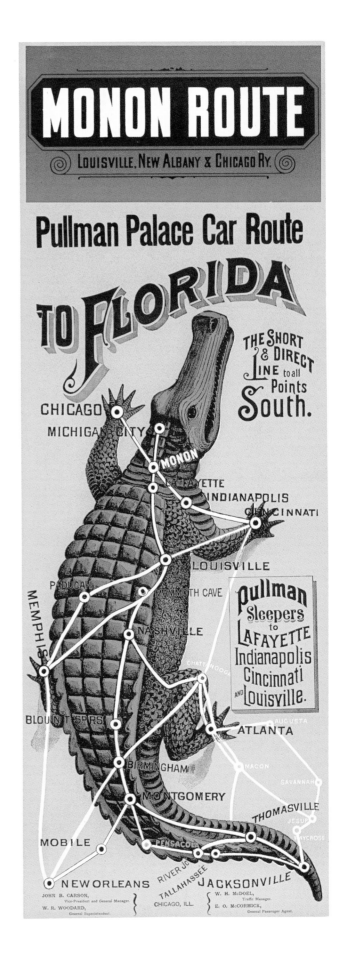

face, Brigham Young's top hat and populous marriage bed, the red man's ceremonies and his wrath, the clear desert air, the wild prairie, the elemental earth whose nearness made the heart beat faster, like the nearness of the sea. The West was beckoning.

—Jorge Luis Borges, *Collected Fictions*

Railroaders generally agreed that maps and calendars did not induce travel but instead offered a constant reminder to those who found it necessary to travel in any event, particularly for business. The decade of the eighties also marked the beginning of the railroads' concerted promotional effort to inspire and increase travel by emphasizing the appeal of place. This occurred with the railroad campaigns that sought to develop the American West. Eastern lines had long promoted scenic destinations and resorts, particularly Niagara and Saratoga; now the western lines amplified that appeal. The change coincided with the completion of the second and third transcontinental routes in 1883.

From the beginning, western railroad promotion focused on changing wealthy Americans' orientation from Europe to the West. It was the decade of the invention of "Wonderland," when a trip west invoked still-fresh memories of pioneer adventure and Manifest Destiny.[12] Still, in an age of crudely rendered advertisements, the railroads relied primarily on the power of the printed word.

Southern Pacific pioneered the campaign to sell the American West. Realizing that wealthy tourists demanded comfortable accommodation, SP built, in a mere one hundred days, an inn that would become the prototype for successful western development. The famed Hotel Del Monte opened June 1880; five years later SP publicists bragged: "No story that can be told of the Hotel Del Monte at Monterey can be overdrawn. It is the handsomest watering-place in America." The railroad convinced the likes of Andrew Carnegie, Andrew McNally, and Joseph Pulitzer to attest to its claim: "The charms of the hotel and climate at Monterey have not been exaggerated; they cannot be. Del Monte has no equal." By 1887 Hotel Del Coronado at San Diego and the Raymond and the Green at Pasadena brought the tourists southward.

Other roads appealed to the West's thrill and spectacle. "In all the world there is no place so beautiful, imposing, sublime and awful, that may be so easily and comfortably visited," began Denver & Rio Grande's evocative description of the ride through Colorado's famed Black Cañon of the Gunnison. It went on to contrast "towering monuments that flaunt the clouds" with the specter of certain disaster: "the train goes sailing straight as the flight of an arrow right at a bronze and ponderous bulwark that looks as if the cars must crash against it and pile up in broken and splintered masses." Such rides did indeed hold tourists spellbound; one reported: "Everybody is too absorbed in wonder to indulge in conversation, and a sigh of relief is heard when [we] emerge from the 'Gorge.'"[13]

Fig. 7. (FACING PAGE) Monon Route, July 1887, 10½" x 28". Arthur Dubin collection.

Fig. 8. (ABOVE) The Alton's first calendar, from an 1883 booklet. Arthur Dubin collection.

Among the earliest examples of large-format advertising that the railroaders used to inspire Americans westward was the oversized landscape photograph. They well understood that photography's claim to accurate depiction of the natural landscape provided a strong sales inducement. The 1880s marked the high point of popular interest in and use of the romantic, awe-inspiring images.

Southern Pacific pioneered the use of photographs as an advertising medium, distributing San Francisco photographer Carleton E. Watkins's California views. The Northern Pacific became known for the more workmanlike productions of Minneapolis photographer F. Jay Haynes. William H. Jackson, of course, produced memorable images for a score of lines. Railroads back East also made notable use of photographs. The Pennsylvania employed Frederick Gutekunst and William Rau to depict its masterful engineering; their images gave strong support for its "Standard Railroad of America" ad claim.

Photographs remained a prime promotional tool for the railroads through the first decade of the twentieth century. As late as 1911, railroad ad man Chas. S. Fee, perhaps the medium's leading proponent, affirmed their pivotal role: "In almost any first class hotel you may enter, and in many offices, you will find California portrayed in magnificent photographic enlargements, superbly framed and hung in conspicuous positions. . . . Though advertisements, they are, nevertheless, among the highest examples of photographic art."[14]

As Southern Pacific's 1886 depiction of the "celebrated winter resorts of California" suggests, by mid-decade the roads had begun to augment their efforts with posters. The line's early poster imagery was quite varied; it depicted scenic destinations such as Yosemite's Mirror Lake, the Big Trees, and Lake Tahoe, and gave evidence of the prominent place the road accorded its "Sunset Route" moniker and logo. SP would use posters more consistently than any other line (fig. 9). By contrast, the songbirds decorating Chicago & North Western's contemporaneous "To the Enchanted Summer Land" exemplified a markedly different but no less dramatic use of nature's appeal (fig. 10).

At about the same time, other lines began to use another variant on the poster, colorful lithographed scenes of well-known destinations along their lines. Michigan Central became known for its depiction of Niagara Falls, Chesapeake & Ohio for the Blue Ridge and Old Point Comfort. Best known of all were the Santa Fe's chromolithographs of the Grand Canyon; the first was produced in 1892, years ahead of its time.

That year, artist Thomas Moran, who had explored and painted the Grand Canyon in 1873–74 as part of the Powell Expedition, revisited the canyon at the railroad's invitation. Moran's romantic lithograph, notable for its contrast of brooding dark depths and brilliant sunshine, offered a range of expression unavailable to still photographers; it was much more evocative and effective in communicating the canyon's diverse moods. In its effort to promote travel to the canyon, the line

distributed the lithograph to teachers and offered it as sales incentive for special excursion tickets and even subscribers to the *Los Angeles Times.* But western tourism as yet appealed primarily to the few who could afford to take their leisure on the Del Monte's veranda; the wagon rides, dirt, and hardship of true adventure were summed up by the popular refrain, "Wouldn't have missed it for the world. Wouldn't go through it again for a thousand dollars!"[15] Another decade would pass before the Grand Canyon and its like became tourist draws (fig. 11).

Fig. 9. (ABOVE) Southern Pacific destination posters, 1886–87; from *Winter Excursions* booklet.

Fig. 10. (FACING PAGE) Chicago & North Western lithograph, ca. 1885, 9¼" x 27". Charles Stats collection.

Fig. 11. (BELOW) *The Grand Cañon of the Colorado,* lithograph, 1892, Gustave Buek after Thomas Moran, 38½" x 22¼". East Hampton Library.

1890s: "Reason Why" Advertising

The decade of the 1890s marked the introduction of the decorative or art poster to American advertising. It also saw a broadening under-

standing and implementation of sophisticated advertising theory. By the early 1890s advertisements were increasingly designed with the objective of "creat[ing] demand and meaningful product differentiation."[16] The adaptation of the art poster's design dictates to the new commercial imperative of product differentiation would define the decade.

The railroad men's use of posters and other large-format advertising reflected this development. In the decade's early years they continued to experiment with a range of large-sized formats, notably billboards and photogravure prints. These pointed to a new trend that aimed to attract patronage by employing broad-based popular appeals. As the decade progressed they endeavored to apply, with varying success, the art poster's dictates of simplicity of design and directness of message to their advertisements. Most frequently their objective was to address their biggest challenge—differentiating a product that was fast becoming a commodity. Ironically for the railroaders, the art poster's influence was felt most in the evolving design of magazine advertisements and booklets, their primary media vehicles.

Perhaps the most important development in railroad promotion as the decade opened was the arrival on the scene in mid-1889 of New York Central & Hudson River's GPA George Henry Daniels (fig. 12). In short order Daniels made himself the most influential man in the business; his example set railroad advertising patterns for nearly two decades. Although he made frequent use of large-format advertisements, he seldom used actual posters. Rather than focusing on the limited traffic potential of resorts and tourism, Central increasingly sought to appeal to the need for mass transportation.

Daniels based his promotional strategy upon the concept of product differentiation. From the first his campaigns focused on the fact that the Central operated the nation's most extensive four-track mainline. Under "The Four-Track Series" brand, he offered for sale, at fifty cents each, a set of photogravure etchings by W. H. Jackson. They depicted scenic spots along the Central's right of way—Horseshoe Falls, Niagara; Washington Bridge; and most famously, "Rounding the Nose," which contrasted Central's modern

Fig. 12. George H. Daniels, 1892.

four-track right of way with the placid Mohawk River and a rustic country road. Daniels's commercial variation on the landscape photograph brought the Central's modern identity into thousands of homes.

Two years later Central drew upon the nation's fascination with speed and technology by inaugurating the *Empire State Express,* which Daniels made famous as "the fastest train in the world." He blanketed the nation with oversized photogravure prints and full-page halftones of the *Express* at speed, while making it clear that the *Express* was primarily a coach train and that everyone could afford to ride like a Vanderbilt. He attached his railroad to the national spirit of Manifest Destiny, promoting the *Express* as the outstanding example of America's emerging industrial might. By 1896 his advertising claim that the "rumble of the Empire State Express is heard round the world" was no overstatement. NYC&HRR president Chauncey Depew displayed a print of the *Empire State Express* above his desk at Grand Central station. Doubtless Daniels's selection of subject and media influenced his peers (fig. 13).

Less sophisticated but more typical were E. O. McCormick's Big Four Route painted signs of 1894, which employed a mix of humor and corporate symbol to gain attention. The series depicted a tramp being pursued by a menacing dog, always under the heading, "Take the Big Four." In each, the tramp sat upon, carried, or rode as a bicycle, a big, red "4" (drawn from the line's well-known calendar logo), while keeping just barely ahead of his pursuer (fig. 14). Advertising man Charles Austin Bates (1866–1936) derided his comic approach as "silly and undignified," suggesting instead that McCormick "give some reason why [his line] is better than the others," that he try to build what would years later be termed brand equity. "The Big Four railroad has a great many advantages to offer," he argued, "and would gain more by stating these advantages in a direct, dignified way than by all the flippantly funny advertising they can publish in twenty-five years."[17]

By 1895, the quest for differentiation had become a trend. Bates, one of advertising's pioneers and an outspoken advocate of advertising reform, addressed the dynamics of product differentiation as applied to railroad service. "Every road has some peculiarity which may be turned to advantage," he asserted: "Find that reason and you have found the point to advertise." The attempt to carry out Bates's formulation defined the railroaders' continuing experiments.[18]

The Lithographed Display Poster

At the same time, the decorative poster had begun to reach limited commercial acceptance, marking the beginning of a brief and heady "age of the poster." Throughout the 1870s and 1880s, popular interest grew in colorful posters by Chèret and other European artists such as Eugene Grasset and Aubrey Beardsley. Chèret's work, in particular, prompted imitation. His genius lay in creating designs that integrated brilliant color schemes with human movement and compelled attention;

Fig. 13. The *Empire State Express* running at 60 miles an hour, full-page magazine halftone, 1892, 15½" x 11".

Fig. 14. (LEFT) Big Four, painted signs, autumn 1894. New York Public Library.

Fig. 15. (FACING PAGE TOP) "Railroad Poster" column heading, *The Bill Poster,* 1896. Duke University Rare Book and Special Collections Library.

Fig. 16. (FACING PAGE BOTTOM LEFT) Pennsylvania Railroad, 1896.

Fig. 17. (FACING PAGE BOTTOM RIGHT) Colorado Midland Railroad, 1896. Duke University Rare Book and Special Collections Library.

throughout the 1880s and 1890s the streets of Paris were filled with his work.

The art poster first appeared in the United States in 1889 when the Century Publishing Company commissioned Englishman Louis Rhead to design posters for display in the windows of the stores that sold its magazines. *Harper's* hired the American artist Edward Penfield in 1893 to do the same, sparking a trend. Penfield and his contemporaries Will H. Bradley, J. C. Leyendecker, and Maxfield Parrish set out to create a more restrained "American" style. They drew upon the American woodcut tradition, emphasized delicate colors, and chose women and flowers as subject matter. Their most popular examples were purely decorative and employed, as one contemporary put it, "something of the Middle Ages, corrected by something of the Japanese."[19] Most were created for competitions held by the publishing houses, which used the winning entries to promote special issues of their leading magazines.

Bicycle manufacturers in particular copied the publishing houses' stylistic and promotional practices. However, in contrast to Britain and Europe, progress in American poster design remained painfully slow.[20] The publishers' new designs had little immediate effect on the railroaders' continuing search for a competitive edge.

Adapting the art poster to commercial ends raised difficult questions about design and function, and sparked controversy among artists and advertising professionals. Louis Rhead argued that the strongest poster designs were purely decorative: "A poster should be essentially design, not a picture," he stated.[21] However, most businessmen agreed with Bates in questioning the advertising value of posters that aimed to be works of art. Bates invoked the characteristically American appeal to the practical: Such advertising, he argued, "doesn't try to appeal to common, every-day people. It aspires to interest only a class and a very small class at that." To Bates's mind, the ideal poster combined artistic values and commercial imperative: "It will have all the striking color and outline effects of the best work, and better still, it will tell in a few terse, pointed convincing sentences the most important facts about the article advertised."[22]

The railroaders' efforts were spurred on by the editors of an innovative new advertising monthly, *The Bill Poster*. When in June 1896 its editors polled a group of railroad leaders about their interest in the poster medium, they were heartened by the reply. The "great majority heartily endorsed the billboard method in the most praiseworthy manner," they reported. Still, most were reluctant to take the lead: "Innovations are distasteful to railroads until competition forces their adoption," explained the editors. Even so, the magazine began a special "Railroad Poster" column with the objective of documenting noteworthy examples (fig. 15). As they had hoped, the railroads responded enthusiastically. Six months later the editors declared the railroad poster indispensable, bragging, "Less than a year ago the railroad poster, as a regular advertising medium for general purposes, was regarded as an experiment, and by many a very useless one at that."

The railroads' productions ran the gamut from the purely decorative to the garish; most fell well short of Bates's ideal. New York Central sought to inspire tourists to visit its signature destination by posting images of Niagara Falls. Central's primary competitor, the conservative Pennsylvania, employed, of all things, a beautiful woman. Its "Poster Girl" of 1896 graced billboards and booklets, holding the line's route map across her bosom, suggesting, "Look at the Map"; judging by her popularity, most travelers' attention was drawn elsewhere (fig. 16). Colorado Midland's *Silver Serpent* poster reflected a circus poster heritage, and featured a huge curling monster set alongside the line's distinctive logo of an Indian brave (fig. 17).

The St. Paul (Chicago, Milwaukee & St. Paul) produced the era's most decorative work, hiring artists William W. Denslow and Ethel Reed to illustrate its motto, "First Class in every respect." Denslow's design sold the carrier's claim of comfort and exclusivity by employing the device of two contrasting scenes. To one side, before a bright red background, Denslow set a solitary, elegantly dressed young woman whose purse carries the St. Paul logo. On the opposite side, colored in monotone gray, a crowd waits amid its piled luggage (fig. 18). In Reed's interpretation, a young lady of almost Parisian demeanor waves a white handkerchief; the St. Paul name, written in large letters, dominates the foreground (fig. 19). Reed, then all of twenty, was thought to be one of

Fig. 18. (LEFT) William Denslow, 1896, 17½″ x 13½″. Chicago Historical Society.

Fig. 19. (ABOVE) Ethel Reed, 1896.

Fig. 20. (FACING PAGE LEFT) J. C. Stubbs, San Francisco, ca. 1890. Union Pacific Historical Collection.

Fig. 21. (FACING PAGE RIGHT) *Sunset Limited* advertising samples, *Sunset* magazine, 1898. New York Public Library.

the most promising of the new crop of poster artists; Denslow would later illustrate L. Frank Baum's book *The Wizard of Oz*. Of the two, Denslow's bold design best communicated the St. Paul's singularity.

Southern Pacific's productions best melded the art poster trend with effective commercial appeal. Its *Sunset Limited* initiative of 1895–98 was the first of the great campaigns that sold California. A super-deluxe winter-season express intended to take prosperous north-easterners to sunny California, *Sunset Limited*'s combination of luxurious speed and comfortable southern route marked the advent of a significant travel improvement—the ability to outrun the seasons in comfort and convenience, as recently pointed out by *Harper's* editor and world traveler Charles Dudley Warner. SP's campaign mixed the lure of the exotic with the "Sunset" moniker and imagery; it gained national recognition and proved the most effective of the early campaigns.

Southern Pacific produced all manner of innovative advertising in support of *Sunset Limited*. Introduced on the New Orleans to San Francisco run in late 1894, *Sunset Limited* was the keystone of an audacious plan to shift transcontinental travel patterns southward, from Chicago to the New Orleans gateway. Its almost immediate popularity stemmed from advertising. John Christian Stubbs, the marketing genius behind *Sunset Limited,* had signed on with the Central Pacific in 1870, just months after its completion (fig. 20). One of the shrewdest traffic men of his day, Stubbs was the first to fully exploit the appeal of place in posters. He blanketed the Northeast with images of *Sunset Limited* soaring across the western sky, in pursuit of the setting sun, California bound.

Southern Pacific sold *Sunset Limited* with a myriad of variations on that theme. The first poster, produced for the train's 1895–96 season, showed a circus influence; it "pictured the train in mid-air shooting over

that portion of the continent it traverses, and typifying, by its comet-like flight, the meteoric speed at which [it] travels," bragged SP publicists. A crescent moon set in a deep blue sky hung over New Orleans and gradually gave way to a rich golden glow in the west. The landscape on the globe below contrasted New England snowfields with California's flower-tinted slopes. Around the borders thermometer readings offered further inducement to travel by displaying concrete proof of the Sunset Route's mild climate (fig. 21).[23]

The poster designed by New York artist William Howell Bull (1861–1940) for the train's third season (1896–97) won the widest acclaim. As SP publicists proudly described it, "a globe is shown floating through space with the Western Hemisphere outward. Brilliant stars dot the purple blackness of the void, among them belted Saturn, and, analogous, a ring encircles the earth formed by the letters S U N S E T L I M I T E D. Over the polar zone the train itself appears, its glittering headlight illuminating the legend 'Famed the World Around.'" The work was awarded first prize at a Buffalo poster exhibition, one of the few railroad productions ever to be so honored (fig. 22).[24]

Bull moved to San Francisco and became the in-house artist for SP and, beginning in 1898, its pioneering booster-magazine venture, *Sunset.* He specialized in illustrations that emphasized the vast, romantic West, numerous examples of which ran as *Sunset* magazine covers and were also produced as newsstand posters. His work dominated the road's advertising output well into the 1920s.

But though SP's campaign proved a brilliant success, other less fortuitously located lines found a more difficult path.

Oscar Binner's Gigantic Images

Perhaps the poster designs produced by Oscar Binner's Chicago engraving studio best exemplified the difficulty of adapting the decorative poster style to the railroaders' commercial needs. Binner personified the adroit men who rode the coinciding booms in commercial illustration, poster design, and billboard design to financial success. His melding of art and commerce exemplified Chicago's self-confident "I Will" motto (fig. 23).

Essentially a marketing specialist, Binner's innovation was in hiring a talented staff of artists whom he directed to create a singular, attention-getting "Binner" style. Binner set out to differentiate his firm on many fronts: He worked closely with clients in formulating marketing strategy, rather than following the longtime practice among engraving houses of producing whatever a client requested. His firm's marketing focus was evident in its slogans: "modernized advertising" and "Binner's 18-story creations." Binner maintained swank offices atop the Fisher Building, then the city's tallest skyscraper, whereas competitors typically worked out of cramped offices in dark and dirty plants. His bread and butter was the marketing of the new wave of branded consumer goods—Pabst beer, Columbia Bicycles, Singer sewing machines. Like the European posters, Binner posters employed bright colors and emphasized the female figure, but his artists were more literal and realistic in their depiction, often adapting the decorative poster style to the billboard's scale. "We simply apply the artistic to the practical," he declared. "In other words, we turn art into dollars and cents."[25]

OSCAR E. BINNER.

Fig. 22. (FACING PAGE) W. H. Bull, 1896–97, 21" x 28". California State Railroad Museum.

Fig. 23. (LEFT) Oscar Binner, 1897.

Fig. 24. (RIGHT) The Lake Shore Girls as depicted on a timetable cover, 1896. Arthur Dubin collection.

Binner's first railroad client, the Lake Shore & Michigan Southern, the Midwest's best engineered and most prosperous line, was not particularly difficult to promote. His studio began with art posters, introducing the "Lake Shore girls"; striking poster images of stylish women in the manner of Will H. Bradley, filled with the long curves and startling swirls characteristic of the Arts and Crafts movement. Produced throughout 1896 and 1897, the images sold comfort, their implication being that the line's matchless roadbed provided the most comfortable route between East and West (fig. 24).

Binner's work for a second midwestern line, the Chicago Great Western Railway, proved a more difficult proposition. It illustrates the challenge of developing a unique, attention-getting selling message under intensely competitive conditions. As the least favorably located of the five lines competing for passenger traffic between Chicago and the Twin Cities, CGW had developed a tradition of aggressive marketing. In 1889 it had followed the lead of competitor Chicago & Alton in adopting a trademark that matched its route to a symbol, advertising itself as "The Maple Leaf Route" and depicting its lines as the leaf's veins. Binner's first poster for the Chicago Great Western dated from 1896 and employed a typical art-poster theme: It set a pretty girl in scenic surroundings and sold on-line resorts. Not surprisingly it went largely unnoticed (fig. 25).

Binner's second attempt, an oversized (eight sheet), thick-lipped caricature of a Pullman porter who promised "the very latest Pullman productions," proved to be resoundingly popular (fig. 26). Pleased,

From the noisy, dusty city / To the country's cool retreat, / Far beyond the grime and bustle, / Far beyond the jar and heat: / 'Mid the long and tangled grasses, / Perfume-ladened woods and nooks,

Noting not the hour that passes, / Just enjoying rest or books; / On the quiet lake then trolling, / Or along some cool stream wading, / With indifference now strolling.

In the sunshine or the shading; / Whence no sound disturbs the stillness / Save the distant cawing crows / And the hours pass by unnoticed / Till the happy evening's close.

CHICAGO GREAT WESTERN RAILWAY TO THE SUMMER RESORTS OF THE NORTHWEST

THE MAPLE LEAF ROUTE

F. H. LORD General Passenger and Ticket Agent ~ Chicago.

Fig. 25. Binner studio, 1896, 20" x 15". Chicago Historical Society.

George Mead, CGW's "college-bred, polished" advertising agent, termed it "a surprisingly cheap [and] very effective means of catching the public eye."[26] Mead subsequently commissioned what he claimed to be the largest railroad poster yet produced. Posted in May 1897, the gargantuan forty-eight–sheet production, headlined "Finest Trains in the West," depicted in three-quarter perspective an entire seven-car passenger train and locomotive (fig. 27). Posted throughout the West from Chicago to Los Angeles, Mead's flyer scored a hit and was followed by a second forty-eight–sheet poster featuring three separate interior views: club car, diner, and luxurious coach seating. Competing roads immediately copied CGW's oversized billboards, starting a trend: Railroaders everywhere thought the gigantic proportions perfect for depicting their new limiteds.

The railroaders' emphasis on passenger comfort is understandable. At best, it took $4^1/_2$ days to cross the United States; comfort *was* of supreme importance. NYC&HRR president Chauncey Depew commented in *The Outlook:* "American travelers will take luxury every time if they can get it without extra cost."[27] Competition, he explained, drove the avalanche of higher speeds and ever more luxurious and elaborate furnishings. Images of speeding locomotives and express trains were pervasive; *McClure's, Harper's,* and other monthlies regularly profiled the latest railroad speed run. Ultimately, popular enthusiasm spurred look-alike poster displays. The gigantic billboards exemplified American pragmatism, business efficiency, and mass production; however, they bore little relation to their more fanciful and imaginative predecessors.

Now the railroads competed to see which could present the largest poster of the latest limited described in the boldest superlatives. Burlington's 1898 board depicted the "Finest Train on Earth"; St. Paul's of 1899 sold its *Pioneer Limited* as "The Only Perfect Train" (fig. 28). The images spiraled out of all proportion to good sense. Other midwestern competitive battles produced the first train to be automatically photographed at speed, 1901's image of *The Burlington's Number One,* and a gigantic $4^1/_2$ by 8 foot photo of the *Alton Limited,* taken with the world's largest camera.[28]

As the railroaders posted, one outspoken railroad advertising agent upbraided his peers for their look-alike productions. Great Northern's W. L. Agnew offered an insightful analysis. "When you see one you see

Fig. 26. (TOP LEFT) Binner studio, 1896.

Fig. 27. (BELOW) Halftone of Binner studio 48-sheet poster. Duke University Rare Book and Special Collections Library.

Fig. 28. (TOP RIGHT) *Pioneer Limited* billboard, 1899. New York Public Library.

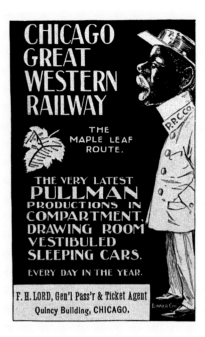

THE "MAPLE LEAF'S" FAMOUS 48-SHEET—THE LARGEST AND FINEST OF MODERN POSTERS.

all," he complained of the "splendid" look-alike "train picture" billboards. "Ninety-nine percent have a picture of a train—a model, modern, vestibuled, electric-lighted, mogul-engined beauty. They are all the 'best on earth,' 'finest on earth'; all 'limiteds' or 'fast mails'; all very pretty, very expensive, very well painted, and all exactly alike. . . . Except for the small trademark and name, the same signs would do for all."

"Yes, they are credible productions by good artists," he continued, but "Advertisements? Oh, no; they are meant to amuse the children and furnish spots of color along the electric car lines." Agnew concluded that most railroad advertising "wasn't worth the money spent on it." He challenged his peers to revisit Bates's formulation: "What railroads need is

advertising that climbs out of the rut and routine, dares to be original, invites attention, compels remembrance. . . . [T]here are points of difference that intelligent, careful study will reveal, and that once found and made use of will make the advertising of that road unique, forceful, paying."[29]

NOTES

1. "Railway Advertising," *Printers' Ink,* Feb. 3, 1892, pp. 147, 148.
2. Norris, *Advertising and the Transformation of American Society, 1865–1920,* 1987, p. xvi.
3. Weill, *The Poster,* 1985, p. 72.

4. *The Artist & Advertiser,* Feb. 1931, p. 5.

5. Presbrey claims first use of the process, appropriately in a railroad booklet.

6. Pratt, *American Railways,* 1903, p. 70.

7. Pratt, pp. 71–73.

8. *Printers' Ink,* June 15, 1892, pp. 787–788.

9. Proceedings of the American Association of General Passenger and Ticket Agents, Sept. 16, 1890, pp. 61–62.

10. *Judicious Advertising,* Feb. 1908, pp. 67–68; the earliest known example displays Alton calendars for 1883 and 1884.

11. *Printers' Ink,* June 12, 1901, pp. 20–22.

12. In 1883 Chas. S. Fee, "ever awake to the advantages of good advertising," coined the seminal moniker "Wonderland" for Northern Pacific's prime scenic attraction, Yellowstone National Park. He ran NP advertising for twenty-one years. *Profitable Advertising,* May 15, 1896, p. 360.

13. *The Inland Printer,* Aug. 1889, pp. 961–963.

14. "How the SP Advertises," *The Graphic Arts,* Dec. 1911, p. 20.

15. *The Christian Union,* Jan. 30, 1892, p. 236.

16. Norris, p. 34.

17. *Printers' Ink,* June 27, 1894, p. 827.

18. "The leading protagonist of advertising reform in the '90's." —Presbrey, *The History and Development of Advertising,* [1929] 1966, p. 310; *Printers' Ink,* Nov. 20, 1895, pp. 65–67.

19. *The Chautauquan,* Jan. 1897, p. 460.

20. Presbrey, p. 496.

21. *Profitable Advertising,* Aug. 15, 1895, p. 70; the editor cited Rhead's comments as published in *The Bookman,* June 1895.

22. *Charles Austin Bates Criticisms,* Aug. 1897, pp. 115–116.

23. *Sunset,* May 1898, pp. 96–97.

24. Ibid., pp. 96–97.

25. *Profitable Advertising,* Aug. 15, 1897, pp. 76–81.

26. *The Bill Poster,* Apr. 1897.

27. *The Outlook,* Oct. 2, 1897, pp. 328–332.

28. *Profitable Advertising,* July 15, 1898, p. 107; *The Inland Printer,* Feb. 1901, p. 799.

29. "On Railway Advertising," *Printers' Ink,* Apr. 5, 1899, pp. 3–4.

TWO   **1900–1909**

That the fine frenzy regarding posters which raged in America some two or three years ago is now . . . a thing of the past there can be no denying.

[But] it is incontestable that the artistic poster is part of America's advertising.

—Percival Pollard, "American Poster Lore"[1]

Advertising Revolution

By 1898 the nation's infatuation with art posters had waned as quickly as it appeared. The railroads' experience reflected that change: *The Bill Poster*'s railroad column had ceased just fourteen months after it began, in August 1897. Although posters and billboards remained an integral element of American advertising, the medium never fully regained the popularity and heightened sense of innovation of the 1890s. The art poster's greatest impact was felt in the broader advertising and printing industries where its legacy marked the advent of modern commercial design.

During the 1890s improved processes of printing and illustration, particularly the refinement of halftone technology, revolutionized the quality of work produced. This trend, together with the art poster's contemporaneous revolutionary influence on design, sparked a boom in commercial illustration. It gave rise to a new sort of art profession, that of commercial artist. Historian Victor Margolin points out that it was a time of artistic challenge and opportunity. "The innovation and experimentation that characterized the best posters of the 1890's was due in large part to the fact that many of the designers were young men and women with no commitment to the academic traditions that preceded them."[2]

The popularization of the decorative poster had also affected attitudes about commercial art. Chicago artist and editor Charles Francis Browne best characterized the new outlook. Browne, a prominent voice in the era's characteristic debate and quest for an "indigenous and genuine" American Art, also pointed to the dynamic role of young, innovative commercial artists who worked with the new technologies in shaping that debate. He singled out J. C. Leyendecker as the personification of the new direction.[3] That the field offered abundant opportunity for creative challenge, personal recognition, and profit soon became incontestable—by 1902 even the likes of Frederic Remington illustrated ads.

Increasing use of mass circulation media—newspapers and magazines—mirrored American advertising's shift away from the poster medium. Advertisers made the change because of their increased reliability and efficiency in reaching potential patrons on a national scale. George P. Rowell, founder of the nation's first ad agency and publisher of the pioneering journal *Printers' Ink,* had initiated the drive for media accountability in the 1880s. His campaign for accurate reporting of newspaper and magazine circulation introduced the *American Newspaper Directory,* the first reliable means of comparing media efficiency, and spurred a movement toward mass circulation media among advertisers intent upon reaching the vast American market.

Rowell's work further shed light on how differences in outlook and scope of markets affected poster development overseas. By contrast British and Europeans lagged in such qualitative measures; at the beginning of the twentieth century they had only begun to take similar action. Of course differences in language and smaller populations and markets also retarded their progress. The net effect of this was that the poster remained the dominant and most efficient medium in Europe and Britain.

Further contributing to the demise of posters was the indiscriminate postering and painting of the nation's walls, barn sides, and scenic venues, which unleashed an anti-poster backlash. Frederick Law Olmsted, Jr., campaigned against "the evils of the abuses of public advertising," as did Central's George Daniels.[4] In 1898, Daniels, by then among the most prominent men in America, joked that "the sign-board advertising business in Europe is so overdone that there is no landscape or peace for the eye." Daniels was dead serious about fighting such excess at home, arguing that for American railroads the "only proper and paying advertising" was in newspapers and magazines.[5] Notably, his particular crusade was against the painting of signs on the Hudson River Palisades, of which his line offered the only view. Daniels's hyperbole aside, the Europeans quickly adopted organized poster displays, or hoardings, while Americans continued to post and paint everywhere.

Overseas developments in poster design also produced interesting parallels which over time became an important point of reference for the railroad men. British advertising commentators offered a timely perspective on American developments, while confirming that across the Atlantic, models of railroad competition also affected poster development. Britain's railways competed for traffic in important markets just as aggressively as American lines. Not surprisingly, the parallel produced striking similarities in advertising strategy. In 1902 the new British trade

journal *The Advertising World* complained of a dull similarity in railway poster displays, asking, "What interest is it to the passenger to see the engine and train which he is likely to travel by?" Instead of the latest locomotives and trains, the editors suggested depictions of foreign ports and scenic spots. They recommended that railroad managers travel to France, where "they may see a Picture Gallery, the like of which cannot be seen throughout the world."[6]

It was in France that the modern railway travel poster was invented. In 1842 the French government organized its fledgling railroad systems into a network of regional carriers with the objective of limiting unproductive competition. Thus the French railways were free to concentrate on selling the attractions unique to their region. Most effective was the Paris Lyons Méditerranée (PLM) whose tracks followed the scenic Rhône Valley past vineyards and lush hills to Mediterranean beaches and resorts. In the decade of the 1880s PLM began to produce and distribute the first travel posters, hiring a range of artists including Chèret. The line became world-famous for its inspiring depiction of brilliant sunsets and mountain lakes, many by artist Hugo D'Alesi (1883–1906). Indeed by 1902 a British writer quipped that the artist was "sometimes called Hugo d'Allez-y, from the fact that he has induced so many thousands of tourists to patronise places illustrated by himself" (fig. 29).[7]

As their overseas counterparts focused on posters, American railroads followed the national pattern, turned increasingly to mass circulation media, and vastly expanded their advertising expenditure. By the turn of the century their media choices in order of importance were newspapers, national magazines, and illustrated booklets. Indeed, as a group, American railroads were among the largest national advertisers; their advertising spending equaled that of other giant consumer-focused businesses—patent medicines, soaps, and breakfast foods.[8]

To reinforce and follow up on their mass media ads, railroads used illustrated booklets, designed to inspire wanderlust. American railroaders put a great deal of creative energy into the booklets, the covers of which increasingly displayed the poster's most commanding feature, color illustration. Booklets, as the railroaders often pointed out, possessed the advantage of time: They could be perused, and dreamt over, in the comfort of one's home. Furthermore, the railroads' organizational network placed an agent in every town, ready to distribute his line's literature to potential patrons.

This media mix was best represented in the selling of California—the single most successful railroad campaign of the late nineteenth and early twentieth centuries. Here the railroad men deftly employed the appeal of place, supplementing black-and-white newspaper and magazine ads with millions of extravagantly produced booklets that depicted natural beauty and bounty. And for a few intrepid roads, posters continued to play an important role—one often overlooked by eastern commentators.

PARIS · LYON · MÉDITERRANÉE

LE LAC D'ANNECY

Fig. 29. *Le Lac d'Annecy,* 1900, typified Hugo D'Alesi's style. Posters Please, Inc.

1900: Urban Display Windows

To go—sometime—to California is the desire more or less ardent, of everybody who has ever thought of going anywhere.
—*Golden State Limited* inaugural booklet, Henry P. Phelps[9]

The twentieth century was marked by increasing middle-class prosperity, a prime effect of which was the rapid expansion of leisure and vacation travel. Competitive pressures drove the railroad men to tap these new markets by opening extensive networks of metropolitan ticket offices to better merchandise their product. The offices' oversized display windows proved perfect for posters; most railroad posters would now be designed for this setting.

The move toward consolidation in product distribution was fostered by an evolution of sophisticated marketing strategy. By the late 1890s, the pace of railroad innovation had slowed: The continual improvements to passenger comfort upon which many lines had based their advertising ceased to be special features as they were gradually adopted by all. "Few great railroads these days have any distinctive advantages over other lines to offer the traveler, so far as comfort *en route* is concerned," commented transportation advertising pioneer Frank Presbrey (1855–1936). Presbrey now suggested that the scenery and resort destinations unique to each carrier afforded the greatest sales potential. "The successful railroad advertisement is the one which most distinctly and indelibly associates in the public mind the name of the road and the territory or cities it reaches," he wrote. "All talk about superior service has become to a great extent airy persiflage."[10]

Presbrey's insight was supported by changes in the nation's demographics, particularly a broadening of the middle class. As the Depression of 1893 receded, renewed prosperity brought a middle class that was flush with disposable income, ready to travel. A Pennsylvania Railroad ad best summed up the optimism: "An era of splendid prosperity is the hope and promise of the times. Money is easy now, and will be easier. There will be leisure for travel and the means to indulge it."[11] The editors of *Town & Country* magazine concurred, introduced a "Vacation Travel Page," and commented on the phenomenon: "Only within the last few years have we really learned to enjoy [summer] properly."[12] Forward-looking railroaders increasingly sought to attract such patronage by romanticizing the allure of exotic destinations and climates, featuring cool Colorado summers and balmy California winters. The railroads now broadened their appeal, constructing tourist cars and opening hundreds of city ticket offices designed to further increase demand.

The variety of routings and accommodations of long-distance travel across the American continent now spawned a new sales venue that soon became the nexus of the American system. By 1903, New York Central advertised a national network of seventy-seven information bureaus. That same year, English railroad man Edwin A. Pratt observed: "In New York there must be (at a guess) at least 100 of such ticket offices along Broadway alone."[13] Each displayed posters, landscape photos, and window hangers describing new trains and resort destinations in the competition to gain the attention of leisure travelers (fig. 30).

Two lines in particular, the Atchison, Topeka & Santa Fe (AT&SF) and the Southern Pacific, acted upon these trends and began to place greater emphasis on the appeal of place. Both roads focused on California and excelled at display-window marketing; it was primarily through their efforts that large format and poster display continued to develop in the pre–World War I period. Their campaigns produced a diverse range of innovative advertising that effectively initiated the "See America First" movement, selling the same mix of antiquity and natural wonder that so attracted their countrymen to Europe.

The Santa Fe's managers were the progenitors of Presbrey's formula of adopting the appeal of place as a means of differentiating their road from its competitors. The Santa Fe's route followed the path of its namesake pioneer trail, passing ancient Native American pueblos and within seventy miles of the Grand Canyon on its way to southern California. Unlike most railroads, the line rarely featured images of trains in its advertising; instead a trip west on the Santa Fe now became an adventure through an "Old New World."

In 1898 the Santa Fe introduced a landmark advertising campaign that sought to broaden the appeal of travel to California by featuring the romanticized depiction of the Southwest and its native inhabitants. Magazine ads promoting its flagship train, the *California Limited*, paired the railway's name with images of Pueblo Indians and their cultural artifacts—Navajo blankets, Hopi katsinas, native women, and children selling pottery. By associating the Santa Fe name with the romantic depiction of Native Americans, the road effectively communicated its southwestern routing, and provided a reason to go there, in a visually more interesting way than the maps of an earlier generation.

Recognizing that travel west was every bit as expensive and costly as to Europe, the Santa Fe used every opportunity to push what would remain for decades a difficult sales proposition. It even turned the threat of war with Spain to its advantage in ads asking: "You have been abroad. You know all about Europe.... Why not see your own great west? Spend your money at home." Early in 1902, the editor of *Pacific Coast Advertising* remarked on the line's increasingly elaborate window displays, noting the "constant attention" drawn by their array of Indian "curios" and paintings of Indian subjects. That same year, AT&SF ads began to headline "First, See America."[14]

The appeal to the romantic adventure of travel met with immediate success. Over the next five years the campaign expanded to include extensive displays of native artifacts and vividly colored paintings of the region and its inhabitants. Santa Fe's advertising agent William H. Simpson used original paintings as his rivals used posters: By 1910 he had acquired some two hundred paintings for display in ticket offices across the nation. Lithographed versions of especially iconic works were also extensively circulated. Images such as Thomas Moran's *Grand Cañon of Arizona* and Frank P. Sauerwein's *First Santa Fe Train* served to reinforce the overall southwestern-themed marketing strategy (fig. 31). "We believe in pictures, for our road furnishes inexhaustible material for them," Simpson declared in 1902. He distributed all manner of images, including lantern slides and framed colored photos of the Grand Canyon. "In the past year we have probably put out 1,000 of these photos," he estimated.[15]

Illustrative of Simpson's sense of design and color was the 1903 lithograph *First Santa Fe Train*, reproduced by US Colortype Company of Denver and distributed by the thousands. When compared to

Fig. 30. (FACING PAGE) New York Central & Hudson
River Railroad Manhattan ticket office, ca. 1902,
displaying landscape photographs and *20th Century
Limited* broadside. DeGolyer Library, Southern
Methodist University.

Fig. 31. (ABOVE) *First Santa Fe Train Crossing Plains*,
Frank Sauerwein, 30" x 50". Burlington Northern
Santa Fe Railway Art Collection.

Sauerwein's original (1901), Simpson's lithograph appears greatly simplified, more graphic in its definition of figures, amplified in color contrast, and now made immediately recognizable (fig. 32).[16]

Southern Pacific, the other dominant carrier to California, followed a similar overall strategy but differed in its execution. SP's displays featured "photographic and lithographic pictures" of California's scenic icons. SP proclaimed Yosemite scenery to be "grander than Switzerland" and graphically communicated the Big Trees' scale with posters that set a giant sequoia towering above Chicago's Masonic Temple or paired with New York City's soaring new Flatiron Building.

The man behind the campaign was E. O. McCormick, who had joined the SP in 1899. In short order McCormick, both colleagues and detractors agreed, made himself "a powerful figure in the development of the Pacific Coast." The editor of the *Los Angeles Herald* declared that "he has done more to advertise California and [its] resources throughout the East than any other railroad man." Now, nearly a decade after producing the Big Four's comical signs, McCormick had matured, and clearly grasped the advertising value of the West's picturesque features.[17]

Handsome, outgoing, and a gifted public speaker, McCormick would direct SP's promotion and development until his death in 1923. Born in 1858 in Lafayette, Indiana, he began his career at the Monon (Louisville, New Albany & Chicago) and, beginning in 1893, consolidated his reputation with the Big Four. The following year a profile in the trade journal *Business* aptly presented him as the embodiment of the adage, "Old men for counsel and young men for war." In fairness, that description characterized many of his peers. He and men such as Northern Pacific's Chas. S. Fee, Santa Fe's Charles A. Higgins, and William H. Simpson pioneered western settlement and promotion.[18]

Fig. 32. Lithograph after Sauerwein, 1903. Rare Book and Manuscript Library, Columbia University.

McCormick introduced color calendars and built SP's booster magazine, *Sunset,* into a publication of national reputation. SP's "Big Tree Calendar" for 1900, illustrated with a halftone of the Fallen Monarch at Mariposa Grove, was printed in three colors on a blue-and-silver embossed background. It proved to be so popular that *Sunset* bragged: "Preparations have been made to issue a million or more copies if needed to meet demand."[19] McCormick commissioned California artists such as Maynard Dixon to design *Sunset* covers and reproduced them as posters. Dixon had been among the earliest American poster designers, creating the iconography of a mythic "West" for the pioneering western journal *The Overland Monthly.* In 1902 he designed a *Sunset* cover that featured a solitary Indian dressed in brilliant red robes. Particularly evocative of the era's outlook, it, too, became an icon of the West (fig. 33).

In an article titled "Why Railroads Advertise Scenery, Climate and Equipment," McCormick summed up his assessment of railroad promotion's thematic appeals: "'Where to go,' 'What to see,' is a distinct demand of the age," he declared, suggesting that the railroad skillfully blends the artistic with the practical. He argued that the vast improvements in railroad comfort and speed since the Civil War now made nature a silent partner in railroad promotion; that scenery had now become a tremendous asset to the railroad man. "If an earthquake leveled Mt. Hood or Mt. Shasta, drained Lake Tahoe, or smoothed out the big cracks in the Canyon of the Colorado, railway stock holders would have a greater grievance than if dynamite wrecked Wall Street. I would rather own the Yosemite or Multnomah Falls than the Waldorf-Astoria. Things worth seeing are prize possessions."[20]

SP's 1904 poster of the *Overland Limited* crossing the Great Salt Lake on Edward Harriman's brand-new twenty-seven-mile Lucin Cutoff, one of the wonders of the age, illustrated McCormick's philosophy. Here W. H. Bull created a design every bit as powerful as the best European images, setting the *Overland* in a sunset haze of blue and pink, its lighted windows reflecting in the lake's shimmering surface. After a decade's practice, Bull had become adept at incorporating railroad engineering feats and the West's romantic appeal into a single attention-holding image (fig. 35).

A third landmark California campaign also made an effective, if brief, use of posters. In the summer of 1902 the new owners of the Rock Island System (CRI&P), the infamous Moore brothers, set out to better acquaint the traveling public with their railroad. They appropriated a record amount for advertising and hired a young man who had made his reputation with the Burlington back in the nineties, but then quit out of frustration with its conservative marketing practices. James M. Campbell next went to work for the Cudahy Packing Company in Omaha, selling bacon, ham, and laundry soap, primarily on billboards. The Moores hired him away for a record salary to direct the advertising of their new Golden State Route and limited train of the same name.

Fig. 33. Maynard Dixon, 1903, 13³/₈" x 23¹/₄". Posters Please, Inc.

Fig. 34. (LEFT) W. H. Bull's 1903 *Sunset* magazine cover depicting the American River Canyon; also produced as a poster.

Fig. 35. (FACING PAGE) W. H. Bull, 1904. California State Railroad Museum.

OVERLAND LIMITED

EXCLUSIVELY FIRST CLASS
ELECTRIC LIGHTED TRAIN
THREE DAYS
CHICAGO and SAN FRANCISCO

UNION PACIFIC
SOUTHERN PACIFIC

OVERLAND LIMITED
CROSSING THE GREAT SALT LAKE CUT-OFF

When the line opened that November, it became the first to compete directly with the Santa Fe in the lucrative Midwest to southern California market.

Campbell produced one of the nation's first integrated multiple-media campaigns. Among other innovations, he introduced the first two-color advertisements to be run in American magazines—a full page printed in red and black, promoting the *Golden State Limited.* He also experimented with posters, hiring the Forbes Lithograph Manufacturing Company of Boston to produce two in the eight-sheet size. Both designs were brightly colored, simple, and strong. The first sold the *Golden State,* picturing a well-dressed couple leaning out over the observation car railing to catch a first glimpse of a California mission in the distance (fig. 36). The second, headlined "Now is Colorado Time!" pictures a family fishing trip just as Dad hooks a big one (fig. 37). In those days, Colorado's mountain climate provided the summertime complement to winter in California. Late in 1902 Campbell contracted for fifty thousand copies of the two to be posted east of Chicago; the large number was indicative of the scale of his campaign. He considered posters essential to catching public attention, declaring: "They increase the potency of other publicity by giving the impression that the road is doing a great deal of advertising. I consider this half the battle."[21] And it worked, he reported a year later: "The CRI&P's traveling representatives judged the two posters to be the best advertising that we have done," adding that they had produced traceable business leads, a rarity in his experience.[22] But Campbell quit after barely two years, out of frustration with operational delays and general mismanagement. "I should say that Europeans were ahead of us in posters," he commented upon returning from a 1906 vacation on the Continent. Campbell went on to manage the advertising of Procter & Gamble's Ivory soap; his successor at the Rock Island declined to continue the poster initiative.[23]

Indeed, much remained to be done. In 1904, Chas. S. Fee, the inventor of "Wonderland," moved to the Southern Pacific and christened his new employer—whose lines ranged from Portland, Oregon southward along California's mission trail and east to New Orleans, and included the original Sierra Nevada crossing—"The Road of a Thousand Wonders" (fig. 38). When, months later, the San Francisco earthquake destroyed SP's advertising archive, the most extensive in the nation, Fee resolved to do even better. "See America First" now became a "movement"—a matter of mass education.

Design in the New Century

With few exceptions American and European poster designers had gone their respective ways as the twentieth century opened. Americans grew increasingly literal in their illustration, emphasizing realistic representation over stylistic technique. Soon, the European-influenced design process—which focused on expressing readily understood con-cepts and symbols with dynamic illustration—disappeared. In many ways Binner's methods—particularly his reliance on the daunting size of his images rather than a focused creative message in order to gain attention—embodied the difference between the European and American models of poster art. Furthermore, America's art and design culture was still embryonic; American advertising design reflected its clients' business model, emphasizing pragmatism and good business sense. This development led to the often-heard criticism that American posters were nothing more than realistic pictures, expanded to monstrous proportions.

Still there were bright spots: On the larger advertising front, matters were improving. "The designs are bolder, more eye catching, more travel-compelling," commented Great Northern's Agnew in 1902 regarding the rails' latest productions.[24] American ad designers now began to integrate illustration and copy into a single focused selling message. Both Presbrey and advertising copywriter Earnest Elmo Calkins credited George Ethridge with introducing what Presbrey termed "pictorial copy"; Calkins termed it "the poster idea, the eye-catching quality [of] advertising art." With the twentieth century, railroads increasingly employed consumer-focused selling propositions: Service scheduled at regular intervals and clean-burning anthracite coal are two noteworthy examples.[25]

Car Cards

One result of the nation's ongoing billboarding controversy was the rise in popularity of a less intrusive medium—car cards, or posters that were placed on both the insides and outsides of streetcars. By nature limited in size, and transitory in the extreme, car cards demanded that illustration and copy be integrated into a single selling idea that registered a split-second impression. The medium's rigor proved beneficial to the railroads, as it forced them to take a creative step forward from the simple depiction of locomotives and trains.

Railroaders made effective use of the medium. The Burlington cards in particular "make a bold appearance and attract much attention," noted *Printers' Ink* in 1901. Printed in solid black with a huge white

Fig. 36. (FACING PAGE) The Forbes Lithograph Manufacturing Co., 1902.

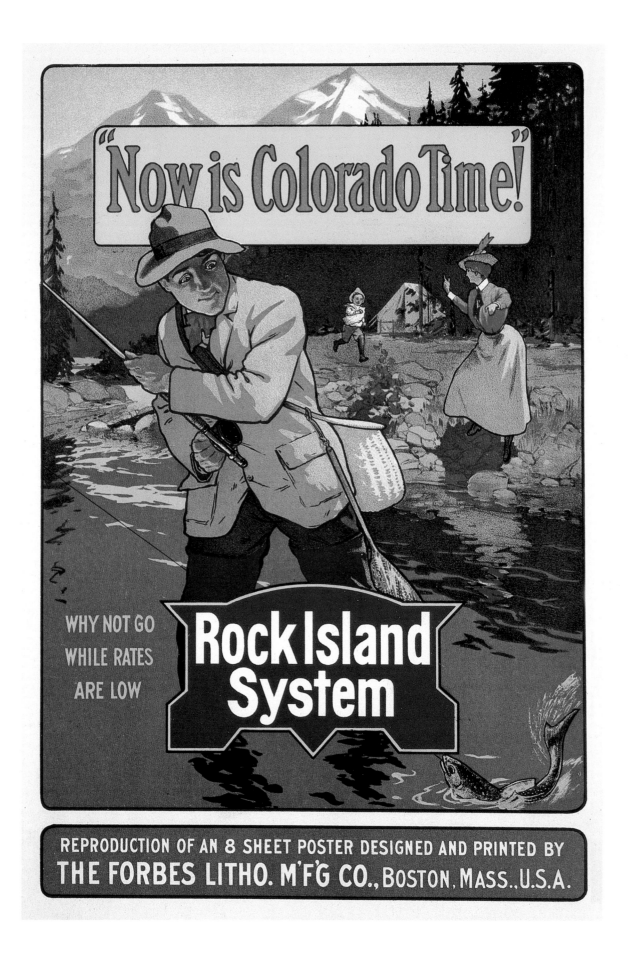

Fig. 37. (FACING PAGE) The Forbes Lithograph Manufacturing Co., 1903.

Fig. 38. (ABOVE) W. H. Bull's 1907 magazine ad depicts an early *Road of a Thousand Wonders* design.

Fig. 39. (RIGHT) Seaboard Air Line ticket-office window hanger, 1903.

circle at the center, the design was meant to suggest a locomotive's head-light; appropriately it had been produced at the direction of J. M. Campbell. A few words of copy went in the centered "headlight," with the road's logos at each corner of the ad (fig. 40). An equally clever Illinois Central card is headlined "Memphis and New Orleans, within easy reach" beneath a photo of a hand enclosing the two cities' names with its forefinger and thumb (fig. 41).[26] Then, in April 1903, the most famous railroad car cards of all appeared.

Of the five lines that competed for New York to Buffalo traffic, only the Lackawanna Railroad used clean-burning anthracite coal. The Lackawanna had begun capitalizing on cleanliness in 1899 by featuring

Figs. 40 & 41. Car cards, 1901. New York Public Library.

passengers attired in white, when its advertising manager W. B. Hunter introduced Mark Twain into the company's advertising. Twain, who lived in Elmira, New York, on the Lackawanna's mainline, was pictured writing a telegram, which read: "Left New York on Lackawanna this AM in white duck suit and its white yet."

Hunter's successor, twenty-two-year-old Wendell P. Colton, who had no previous practical advertising experience, came up with the inspiration to dub his line "The Road of Anthracite" and to present the theme in advertising copy written entirely in rhyming verse. Colton's initial series of car cards, based on the nursery rhyme, "The House that Jack Built," the heroine of which was a girl in white—"all in lawn"—appeared in New York in the summer of 1902. Rhyming advertisements were popular at the time and the reaction to these was extraordinary. The series that followed a year later caused a sensation. Copywriter Earnest Elmo Calkins had named the girl Phoebe Snow and written a second set of jingles in which she describes her trip (fig. 42). Created to mimic the cadence of wheels against rail joints as a train accelerates, the series began:

> Says Phoebe Snow,
> About to go
> Upon a trip
> To Buffalo:
> "My gown stays white
> From morn till night
> Upon the Road
>   of Anthracite."

"It is safe to say that everyone who reads has heard the name 'Phoebe Snow,'" Calkins proudly recalled a few years later.[27] Phoebe became one of the most memorable advertising ideas of the era. By 1904 her image appeared in every possible medium: newspaper and magazine halftones, painted signs, even single-sheet posters. Calkins built a career upon the campaign and the Lackawanna continued the verses for over a decade. However, from a design standpoint, the cards were hardly innovative. They depicted realistic, brightly colored paintings of scenes along the Lackawanna, which artist Harry Stacy Benton made from photographs. More than anything it was the catchy rhyming jingles that proved popular with the public.

Other roads also produced noteworthy poster work in the new century's first years. In 1902, Chicago Great Western Railway demonstrated the powerful innovation of electric lights by posting a nighttime scene of a train, its interior lights all aglow, passing a group of men gathered around a campfire (fig. 43). The Philadelphia & Reading introduced a schedule that was easy to remember in advertising a new hourly service between New York and Philadelphia—"Every time the clock strikes." Its 1903 two-sheet poster, which was intended for posting in Philadelphia, showed Father Time, a clock dial, and a vestibuled train,

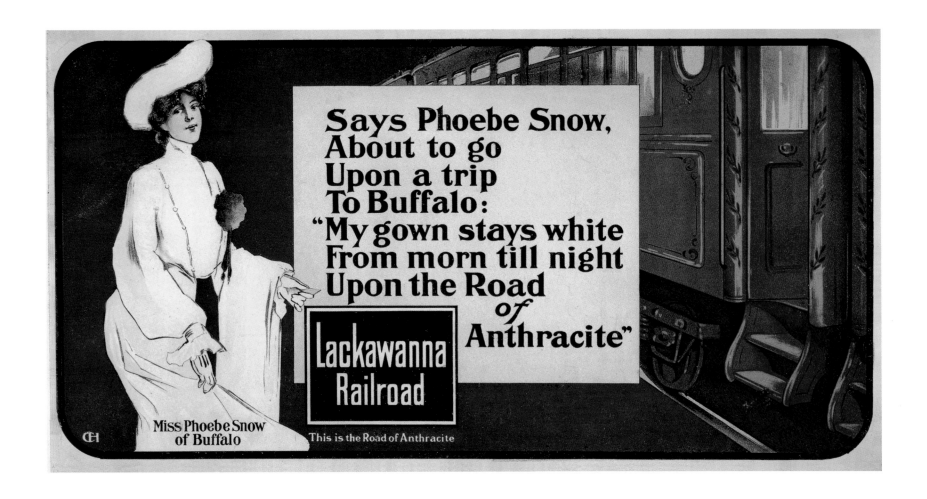

Fig. 42. The first *Phoebe Snow* car card, 1903; 11" x 21".
Railroad Museum of Pennsylvania, Pennsylvania
Historical and Museum Commission.

1900–1909

all offset by a golden background, from which rose the Manhattan skyline. Jersey Central's complementary two-sheet, "Every Hour on the Hour," intended for posting in New York, showed Father Knickerbocker handing a train to Quaker Philadelphia. The two posters caused such a sensation, reported *Printers' Ink,* that the editor of the *New York Journal* featured the designs in its editorial cartoons (figs. 44, 45).[28]

Fig. 43. (ABOVE) *Electric Lighted Trains,* 1902, by Barnes-Crosby. New York Public Library.

Figs. 44 & 45. (RIGHT TOP AND BOTTOM) Car cards, 1902–1903. New York Public Library.

NOTES

1. Pollard, "American Poster Lore," *The Poster,* Mar. 1899, p. 123.

2. Margolin, *American Poster Renaissance,* 1975, p. 46.

3. "The Editor" column, *Brush & Pencil,* Dec. 1899, pp. 143–144.

4. "One flagrant and easily corrected abuse is the indiscriminate painting and placing of advertisements, chiefly upon rocks, trees, fences, etc. . . . by irresponsible advertisers. . . ." *Brush & Pencil,* Sept. 1900, p. 248.

5. *Printers' Ink,* Apr. 13, 1898, p. 35.

6. *The Advertising World,* July 1902, p. 98; Sept. 1902, p. 218.

7. *The Advertising World,* Sept. 1902, p. 218.

8. Historian Presbrey counted railroads among the top four categories of national advertisers (patent medicine, soap, breakfast foods, railroads); *History,* p. 364. By 1892 larger lines typically spent $100,000 or more on advertising; PRR and UP managed over $200,000; approximately a dozen U.S. firms spent more (*Printers' Ink,* Sept. 14, 1892, pp. 307–308). Among railroads, *Printers' Ink* named Northern Pacific "the king of advertisers" (Feb. 3, 1892).

9. Phelps, *Golden State Limited* inaugural booklet, Nov. 1902.

10. *Profitable Advertising,* June 15, 1899, pp. 37–38; *Printers' Ink,* Jan. 14, 1903, p. 26. Presbrey well understood the dynamics of American rail competition and product differentiation. He had graduated from Princeton in 1879, cut his teeth out West in the early eighties on the Santa Fe and Denver & Rio Grande, and ran the leading transportation ad agency. Prominent clients were North German Lloyd (for whom he produced early ship posters), Compagnie Generale Transatlantique, Pinehurst, and Raymond & Whitcomb.

11. *Life,* Christmas Number, Dec. 1, 1898.

12. *Town & Country*'s "Hotel and Travel Bureau" introduced May 1902; editorial, July 12, 1902, p. 16.

13. Pratt, p. 74.

14. AT&SF wartime ads ran May–June 1898; *Pacific Coast Advertising,* Mar. 1902, p. 5.

15. *Printers' Ink,* Dec. 10, 1902, p. 30.

16. The lithograph is reproduced in *The Inland Printer,* Mar. 1903, opposite p. 896.

17. *Southern Pacific Bulletin,* Nov. 1923, p. 8; *Pacific Coast Advertising,* Nov. 1901, pp. 14–15.

18. *Business,* Mar. 1894, p. 108.

19. "Publisher's Page," *Sunset,* Feb. 1900, p. 167; *The Inland Printer,* June 1900, p. 406.

20. *Pacific Coast Advertising,* Jan. 1904, pp. 5–7.

21. *Printers' Ink,* Dec. 10, 1902, p. 10.

22. *The Billposter and Distributor,* Oct. 1903, p. 9.

23. *Judicious Advertising,* Sept. 1905, p. 47; Sept. 1906, p. 62.

24. *Advertising Experience,* Feb. 1902, p. 7.

25. Presbrey, p. 527; E. E. Calkins, *"And hearing not—,"* 1946, p. 169.

26. *Printers' Ink,* Feb. 6, 1901, p. 58.

27. *Printers' Ink,* Dec. 23, 1908, p. 8.

28. *Printers' Ink,* July 22, 1903, pp. 6–7.

THREE   **The Teens**

Realistic art had reached a dead level of excellence. It was no longer possible to make an advertisement striking, conspicuous and attractive by still pictures and realistic groups, however competently painted. Modernism afforded the opportunity of expressing the inexpressible.

—Copywriter E. E. Calkins[1]

Emerging Corporate Imagery

During the decade of the 1910s the nation's railroads experienced the first ill effects of regulation: stagnating growth and diminished access to capital. To boot, the decade saw the automobile transformed from a rich man's toy into a fierce competitor for local and resort traffic. By the economic downturn of 1913 things had gotten so bad that even the New York Central ceased all national advertising. Still, America's western expansion continued full tilt. California's Panama Pacific Expositions of 1915 provided ample promotional opportunity to lure thousands west. While some ran cartoons forecasting overcrowded national parks, the reality was best summed up by a piece in the popular humor magazine *Judge,* titled "See Europe First."

> Friend (at bookstore)—"Hello, old man! Buying a book?"
>
> Other one—"Yes, my wife's going to Europe and she wanted me to get her a volume about the famous historical places in the US, so that she will be able to describe them to the foreigners she will meet."[2]

On the advertising front, the decade further marked the advent of inexpensive color-process magazine advertising and an increasing emphasis on design. One immediate result was the beginning of the decline of the railroaders' beloved booklet medium. The railroads' oversized landscape photos also faced diminished appeal as photography became more widely available. And, once again, posters began to gain prominence.

European developments continued to provide a defining point of reference. Poster design changed dramatically in 1906–1907 when Berlin artist Lucian Bernhard created the *Sachplakat,* or object poster, a simple picture of the item for sale. Convention had followed Chèret's example of depicting beautiful women, but now Bernhard paired a simple picture of the item for sale with equally spare text; an approach that demanded an absolute mastery of drawing, stylization, and composition. Bernhard's contemporary Ludwig Hohlwein also designed equally simple and rigorous compositions, setting one or two figures in the poster's foreground against a uniform background to make them stand out. Both artists used bold color without outlines and emphasized distinctive typography.[3]

The modern German poster greatly influenced American commercial art. Examples filled advertising and design magazines, particularly *The Poster* and *The Inland Printer,* from 1915 to 1917. The style's bold use of color resonated with commentators: "Give us color, . . . more color, and let [it] be laid on in smashing big flat surfaces," urged one. Others pointed to its simplicity of treatment, arguing that its strong, bold outlines registered more effectively than the typical finely modeled, detailed drawings.[4]

That the change soon affected travel posters was evident in the groundbreaking designs produced by the London Underground. Beginning in 1910, ad manager Frank Pick commissioned the best artists of the day to convey a new pictorial message—that one could travel cheaply and comfortably to many London amenities of which one might have been unaware. The Underground designs used simple, focused images of destinations and engaged the imagination; they made Londoners conscious of the wonders of their city. Pick's emphasis on simplified imagery and message had the further effect of cementing the stylistic move away from the traditional travel poster convention of depicting multiple small views. Soon thereafter, British railway campaigns—particularly the Great Western's—began to win notice for their creativity in the American ad press.[5]

Meanwhile, in the United States, the unprecedented success in mass marketing of the automobile set events on another path. Automobile production rose by 800 percent between 1910 and 1916 and led to an explosion in the number of huge driver- and road-oriented billboards. Now twenty-four–sheet poster productions, measuring more than 8 feet tall and 30 feet long, became the norm. "The 'circulation' that grew with the spread of the automobile gave outdoor display a new importance," Presbrey recalled. However, the American billboard remained the realm of realistic, slogan-driven design.[6]

As Americans embraced the automobile, a few railroads experimented with billboards; but most continued to use single-sheet posters, the size best suited to city ticket-office display. Indeed, because the display window remained an integral part of the railroads' promotional plans, its importance as a creative incubator for the single-sheet poster increased.

By and large, the few lines that tried billboards continued to focus on practical advantages rather than engaging notions. A 1913 Northern Pacific campaign best illustrated this approach. When NP, well known for its excellent dining-car service, introduced a dozen billboards advertising its signature "Great Big Baked Potato," the posted image was that and nothing more—a huge baked potato topped with melting butter (fig. 46). The rationale, according to ad manager J. N. Stewart, was "the old adage that 'the quickest way to a man's heart is through his stomach.'" The big spud's inventor, dining-car steward Hazen J. Titus, had encountered a good deal of management resistance to the unconventional appeal. His reply, "Which does NP want, dignity or passengers?" summed up the pragmatic approach. By contrast, a contemporary poster for Britain's Great Western Railway advertised its dining-car service with an image of a farm girl tossing seed to several contentedly well-fed ducks (fig. 47).[7]

The Power of Symbol: Louis Treviso's Santa Fe Posters

Of all the railroads, the Santa Fe made greatest use of the German poster style. Beginning in 1913 the line produced a series of posters that were thoroughly modern in their simplicity of design and integration of corporate symbol with sales message. The posters were part of a groundbreaking marketing campaign that influenced American advertising for decades.

The ever-expanding California boom provided the genesis of Santa Fe's involvement with poster art. The line had begun to use billboard-sized posters in California shortly before the turn of the century, where its most memorable displays featured the "Kite Shaped Track," an excursion train route that traced a figure eight through San Gabriel Valley's orange groves. Others were reminiscent of Southern Pacific designs, displaying the *California Limited*'s name in huge block letters strung across the southwestern sky. Still Santa Fe waited until 1913 to fully embrace the medium. A well-received poster for its crack flyer, the *Santa Fe de-Luxe,* began the story.

An extraordinary demand for premium California accommodations had prompted the line to introduce the *Santa Fe de-Luxe* in November 1911. Modeled on the record success of the *20th Century Limited*, the new flyer cut scheduled time, limited its space to sixty passengers, and charged a grand $25 extra fare. Two years later—in order to better reach the busy, prosperous customers, "who didn't have the time to read the advertisements in a newspaper or a magazine," explained AT&SF advertising manager William H. Simpson, the line set up a dozen brightly colored twenty-four–sheet billboards in Chicago.

Simpson viewed the billboards as an experiment. A pioneer in setting marketing strategy and measuring advertising efficiency, he knew his audience well, and he relied upon ads in magazines and newspapers to lure the great middle class to California; posters, he claimed, could never reach so many so effectively for so little. Yet attracting the wealthy

Fig. 46. (ABOVE) Northern Pacific billboard, 1913.

Fig. 47. (LEFT) Great Western Railway, 1913.

proved a more complex matter; now he expressed the opinion that billboards best appealed to the richest and poorest classes, which no other form of advertising reached efficiently.

Simpson, who allowed that he followed French and German poster art, chose a surprisingly traditional design (fig. 48). He employed the time-tested appeal of comfort, depicting a family at ease in a luxurious drawing-room suite. His poster made no reference to the line's well-known southwestern imagery. Text was limited to the train's name; its famous motto, "extra fast, extra fine, extra fare"; and its destination, "California." Reaction was immediate and overwhelmingly positive, reported Simpson, who recorded himself a convert to the poster medium.

Fig. 48. *Santa Fe de-Luxe* billboard, 1912.

"The next poster we get out," he predicted, "will contain three or four colors commingled to catch the eye and then the slogan that will tell the story."[8]

At the same time, early in 1913, Carlton J. Birchfield, manager of the line's Los Angeles advertising office, hired commercial artist Louis Treviso, age twenty-five, to design posters and newspaper advertisements for the *de-Luxe*. Treviso's work set a new Santa Fe style and made for him a national reputation as a master of layout and lettering.

Treviso created a startlingly modern series of designs that communicated both the trains' comfort and the Santa Fe brand. His simple, direct layouts integrated the line's distinctive cross-shaped logo with whimsical drawings, amplified by brief, distinctively hand-lettered text. His choice of subjects, most famously a gentleman with his feet up on a cushion and a butler in formal attire, effectively communicated the feeling of well being and contentment that the train's name implied (figs. 49, 50). Designed for reproduction in black and white for reasons of economy, the posters stood apart from the highly colored clutter characteristic of the era's billboard displays. The campaign proved so successful that Treviso was soon dubbed "the Santa Fe poster genius."[9]

By spring 1914, Birchfield expanded Treviso's subject range to include the line's traditional southwestern themes. That summer, he also hired a second young artist, Oscar Martinez Bryn. Bryn, whose

Figs. 49 & 50. (ABOVE) Louis Treviso, 1913. Arthur Dubin collection.

Fig. 51. (FACING PAGE TOP) Louis Treviso, 1916; note unique Hopi-inspired frame.

Fig. 52. (FACING PAGE BOTTOM) Louis Treviso, 1915.

ads began to run that June, closely followed Treviso's style, although his illustrations were more detailed. A locomotive raced through wheat fields, headlong into a large logo, to sell "Back East Excursions"; for the *de-Luxe*, he drew a single oversized peacock plume.

Urged on by the trail-blazing Birchfield, the two artists turned to color posters in 1915, beginning a revolution in the depiction of natural wonder and romantic adventure. Treviso framed the line's famous Grand Canyon vista with dark outlines of ponderosa pine trees that grow along the rim, carefully setting a huge logo in the foreground (fig. 51). As did the German artists, he formed his images solely from masses of color, without outline. He designed posters of Hispanic maidens in traditional costume, veiled, holding fans, dancing, celebrating California. He recast the Santa Fe's even then famous image of a Navajo weaver at his loom (fig. 52). Again, the Santa Fe logo figures large and copy was kept to a minimum. He painted with bold colors—orange, blue, yellow, black—and set his images against monotone backgrounds. When Treviso's posters first appeared in Chicago in October 1915, the billboard trade journal *Signs of the Times* urged other artists to go see his work. Its editor subsequently dubbed him "Treviso, the wonder letterer, [whose posters] are causing 'em all to take admirable observation."[10] *The Inland Printer* concurred: "[His] style is strong, virile and interesting without going to the extent of freakishness which some 'modern art' artists do."[11]

A bold diagonal, contrasting the colors of sky and earth, divides Bryn's design for a Hopi Snake Dance poster (fig. 54). In the foreground a ceremonial dancer seems to perch upon a Santa Fe logo as if it were a unicycle. Bryn painted Yosemite waterfalls, California golfers, and motor tourists, that were every bit as vivid and alluring as Simpson's finest landscape painting. Bryn in particular was influenced by Hohlwein. His composition was simple and rigorous, with one or two figures placed in the foreground against a uniform background for stronger contrast. *The Poster* commented that his designs were "shorn of unessential detail; notable for their strength, pleasing color combinations and consequent selling value." "While the brilliant colors of the first few were quite a shock," another client declared, "they are now welcomed and expected."[12]

Unfortunately, original color examples of the artists' early poster work no longer survive. The circumstance is due to their scarcity—they were intended to be one of a kind. Following his now well-established pattern, ad man Simpson displayed the poster designs as if they were paintings, featuring the originals in ticket-office windows rather than reproducing them as single-sheet posters. He even commissioned Treviso to design a special Hopi-inspired frame for his first Grand Canyon work.

Color examples of the artists' advertising work do still exist. A sample that Treviso designed to promote his work for the Los Angeles printers Young & McCallister, in 1916, provides vibrant evidence of his

eye-catching use of color (fig. 55). A series of poster stamps produced for California's 1915 Panama Pacific Expositions provides an example of Bryn's design and palette in miniature, and a booklet-sized version of Bryn's Snake Dance poster provides evidence of its likely coloring (fig. 56).[13]

The two artists and railroad ad man Birchfield fell into an enduring friendship. Treviso's story is particularly compelling. Of Spanish and Mexican heritage, he was born in 1889, in a covered wagon between Casa Grande and Florence, on an Arizona desert trail. He showed an early talent for lettering and at age fourteen moved to Los Angeles to make his living. By 1909 he was working as a sign designer in New York City, where he was one of ten artists specially invited to participate in a

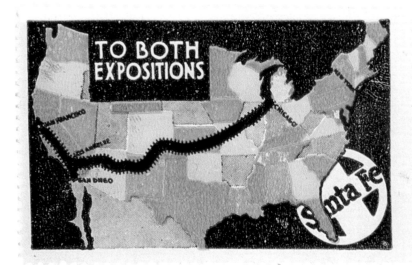

Fig. 53. (FACING PAGE TOP LEFT) Posters, 1917, by
Louis Treviso, top left and bottom center; Oscar Bryn,
top right.

Fig. 54. (FACING PAGE BOTTOM LEFT) Oscar Bryn, 1917.
Sales agent booklet, 8½" x 11", depicting possible
color scheme of original poster.

Fig. 55. (FACING PAGE BOTTOM RIGHT) Louis Treviso,
1916, 3" x 4½". New York Public Library.

Fig. 56. (ABOVE) Oscar Bryn, 1915.

centenary poster competition in Newark, New Jersey. When he returned to Los Angeles, the Santa Fe became one of his first clients and made his career. His resumé of a decade later claimed "Developed Santa Fe Railroad poster and style for newspaper advertising." In 1920 he moved to San Francisco to become art director of the Honig-Cooper Company (fig. 57).

Born in Honolulu in 1883, Bryn grew up in Alameda, California and started out in the art departments of various San Francisco and Los Angeles newspapers. Early in 1914 he "broke away," as he put it, to freelance, first in Los Angeles, and, after a year, in Chicago. There he opened a studio in the Railway Exchange—the same building that housed the AT&SF headquarters. Bryn, whose work well represented the decade's change from simple illustration to designed sales appeal, was an outspoken critic of the marginalization of the artist's viewpoint in advertising. The objective of advertising illustration, he argued, was to create a vivid impression rather than a simple representation. "There are very few instances where illustration in an advertisement so clearly presents the subject advertised that the subject is sold on the strength of the representation," he commented. His posters did just that. Friend Treviso termed him "the most original layout designer in the country."[14] For two decades Bryn headed art direction at leading ad firms, beginning with Erwin Wasey, a pioneering multinational ad agency of the 1920s and 1930s. He continued to paint for the Santa Fe on a freelance basis through the early 1950s (fig. 58).

Still, of the two, it was Treviso who set AT&SF advertising style. "He made of lettering an art as responsive to his touch as music to a Beethoven," began a typical accolade. Others credited him with inventing the "Western" style of advertising, which enjoyed broad popularity during the twenties and thirties. Bay Area artist Paul Carey (1904–2001), who had just begun working as a commercial artist in San Francisco in the mid-1920s, recalled

Treviso's commanding artistic presence some seventy years later: "A highly advanced, unusual and quite brilliant man." The two met when Carey was just starting out on a commercial career. "Unusual individual, Mexican, of course, . . . Louie had a striking sense of color . . . simple, direct, striking . . . unforgettable; he was also kind of wild [the two almost got into a fist fight]. He worked with complete simplicity; knocked everyone else over." Carey credits Treviso as mentor and prime inspiration to many, including himself, Fred Ludekens and, to a lesser extent, Maurice Logan. Carey confirms both the influence of the German poster style in the teens and the consensus that counted Treviso as the leading commercial artist of his day. He also points out that his vibrant color and sense of style stood apart in an advertising world that was (yet) overwhelmingly black and white.[15]

To be fair, Treviso's work benefited from a corporate tradition of producing innovative, eye-catching graphic design. For nearly two decades, the Santa Fe ad men had refined their imagery of the romantic Southwest, distilling it into a distinctive style that dominated a printed page. During 1901 and 1902 Simpson, in collaboration with Chicago artist Carl Newland Werntz, had made dynamic illustration (usually of Indians), distinctively styled hand lettering, and the line's new logo the three integral elements of its designs.[16]

The prominence Treviso gave to the Santa Fe logo indicates that he

Fig. 57. (LEFT) Treviso (6), Oscar Bryn (3), and Carl J. Birchfield (4) in Chicago, 1924. New York Public Library.

Fig. 58. (ABOVE) Oscar Bryn, 1924; poster in background depicts Pullman cars. New York Public Library.

understood the growing importance of brand recognition in a competitive marketplace. In doing this he took the German model a step further, making the logo an integral part of his designs. The British monthly *The Advertising World* underscored the move's significance, commenting, "The manner in which the symbol of the advertisers is given all possible prominence without any detriment to the design will be noted."[17] It is also noteworthy that his work rated the rare honor of reproduction and comment in the British advertising press.

In his capacity as art editor of the trade journal *Western Advertising,* Treviso brought an early focus to western advertising art and design, spearheading a loose association of artists who sought to develop a western commercial art distinctive from that of the East Coast and Europe. "Commercial art in the West typifies all of the best there is in art anywhere," he declared. "The West is a land of romance, local color, adventure, freedom, originality and all those things that enter into real Americanism. It is far enough removed from the influence of Europe to develop a flavor all its own."[18]

Sadly, Treviso's career was cut short by his death from Hodgkin's disease in October 1928, at age forty. Hal Stebbins, publisher of *Western Advertising,* best summed up his career: "As well known as Treviso was for his lettering he had established a superior claim to eminence through his marvelous sense of design, proportion, form, [and] balance." Stebbins's tribute closed with a photograph of Treviso drafting at his studio desk; appropriately, the layout before him is a design for the Santa Fe, showing the AT&SF logo, a warbonneted Indian chief's profile, and the headline "East." "His work with the Santa Fe was the delight of artists everywhere, and no artist was ever more widely copied," remembered *Signs of the Times.* His distinctive style of layout, hand lettering, and Grand Canyon and Navajo weaver poster images became Santa Fe Railway advertising icons, to be recast by later artists for the next thirty years (fig. 59).[19]

Unfortunately, the disruptions of the First World War ended the two artists' remarkable collaboration. The subsequent federal control of U.S. railroads, from early 1918 until March 1, 1920, forced the discontinuance of advertising by individual railroads. The Santa Fe, however, remained railroading's foremost proponent of the pictorial poster.

NOTES

1. E. E. Calkins on design, *"And hearing not—,"* p. 239.
2. "See Europe First," *Judge,* Jan. 18, 1913.
3. Weill, *The Poster,* 1985, pp. 100, 107–110.
4. *The Poster,* May 1917, pp. 49, 50.
5. *Printed Salesmanship,* Oct. 1925, p. 135.
6. Presbrey, p. 560; p. 503.
7. *The Poster,* Sept. 1913, p. 33; *Printers' Ink,* Feb. 17, 1916, pp. 17–25; *The Poster,* June 1913, p. 52.
8. *The Poster,* Jan. 1914, p. 17.
9. Although run initially as newspaper ads during March 1913, the *de-Luxe* designs became famous as posters.
10. *Signs of the Times,* Oct. 1915, p. 29; Feb. 1917, p. 19.
11. *The Inland Printer,* Oct. 1916, p. 71.
12. *The Poster,* Apr. 1917, pp. 28–31.
13. Shown in Young & McCallister, *The Needle.*
14. *The Poster,* July 1916, p. 62; *Western Advertising,* Apr. 1924, p. 42.
15. The authors are indebted to Paul Carey for sharing his recollections in telephone conversations in May 2001.
16. *The Poster,* July 1917, p. 87.
17. The AT&SF logo, adopted in 1901, was a cross meaning "Holy Faith" in a circle representing a wheel, or transportation (Simpson's words).
18. *Western Advertising,* Jan. 1921, p. 29.
19. *Western Advertising,* Oct. 1928, p. 6; *Signs of the Times,* Nov. 1928, pp. 106, 107.

Fig. 59. Louis Treviso drafting; Santa Fe Railway Indian artwork on desk. New York Public Library.

FOUR   The 1920s

Sell them Scenery, Not Plush Chairs.

—Ivor Fraser, publicity manager,
London Underground

Railroad Advertising Transformed

As advertising by individual railroads resumed after the war, only the Santa Fe and Southern Pacific produced posters in quantity. To its credit, Southern Pacific had even managed to evade the wartime advertising ban by producing a patriotic war poster that quoted Woodrow Wilson's vow: "The world must be made safe for Democracy!" New York artist Louis Fancher's boldly rendered design depicted an American eagle with wings outspread, beneath which a locomotive bore down upon a Hun whose helmet sprouted horns (fig. 60).

The decade of the twenties was one of contrasts for the nation's railroads. It marked both the apex of long-distance travel aboard the overland limited train and the beginning of an irreversible decline in railroad passenger loadings and revenues as the nation turned to automotive transportation. The rapidly expanding highway network and the increasing mobility and economy it afforded had the further effect of producing a boom in roadside billboards; twenty-four–sheet posters now ruled American display advertising. Conversely, with few exceptions, the railroads continued to use the single sheet, intended for station and ticket office display.

As the decade opened, the railroads resumed advertising as they always had, despite mounting traffic losses. Their complacency stemmed from the comforting fact that although unprofitable short-haul traffic was in steep decline, long-distance first-class travel, as reflected by Pullman ridership, continued to hold steady (as it would throughout the decade). As a result, they continued to advertise speed, luxurious equipment, and comfort—the "service" factors that they

48

Fig. 60. Louis Fancher, 1918, horizontal half-sheet, 19¼" x 26¾". Swann Galleries.

traditionally deemed appealing to Pullman passengers. Critics charged that the railroad men's outlook bordered on the myopic—that they placed too much emphasis on rail rivals while neglecting to meet the new automotive competition. "We can see that conditions exist where 'service' advertising may be necessary," one ad man wrote in consternation, "but . . . good service is to be expected and should not be advertised as if it were some extraordinary accomplishment."[1]

As the decade progressed and prosperity increased, the shift to the auto could no longer be ignored: U.S. auto ownership more than doubled from 9.3 million in 1921 to 20.1 million in 1927, a 116 percent increase; at the same time the rails lost approximately 20 percent of their passenger revenue. What SP ad man K. C. Ingram termed "the largest factor in decrease of local business" now threatened the rails' bread and butter.[2] Among the loudest voices advocating an aggressive response was the advertising press, which abounded with editorial articles urging the railroads to meet the new competition by varying their message. From the first, the ad men had cited the European and British railway poster campaigns then being renewed with the return of peace. Art historian Carl J. Weinhardt points out that European art trends were never far from the American art world's attention; this was very much the case with railroad poster art in the 1920s. The Europeans' splendid work, widely reproduced and exhibited across the United States, gradually inspired the railroaders to action.

However, the change did not come about readily. When in 1920 the French Railways mounted a well-received poster exhibition that toured the United States, the industry reacted cautiously. Only the New York Central deemed it (marginally) noteworthy, and reproduced a representative selection in its employee magazine, as "a worthy goal to which American poster artists can aspire." The posters sold "the idea of travel," noted C. Philip Russell, author of *The Art of the Poster*, rather than attempting to advertise the merits of a particular line, as was the American custom. He argued that it was well past time for other carriers to join the AT&SF and the SP in producing posters that depicted America's scenic wonders. "How seldom do we see these glories pictured in such a way as to stimulate the appetite for travel, to see if the original is really up to the sample?" he asked.[3]

Remarkably, the Santa Fe's and Southern Pacific's posters were still largely ignored by the eastern press, which thereby displayed its own lack of initiative. In contrast to their innovative work, the Europeans were not that far ahead. The popular French posters, best exemplified by artist Roger Broders's geometric designs and bold color effects for the PLM, had only just begun to register notice. Moreover, the British railways' renewed interest in scenic posters dated from 1923's reorganization of Britain's railways into regional networks, following the French model, with the intent of fostering cooperation rather than competition. That revision gave rise to a new generation of marketers committed to the melding of art and advertising, best personified by London &

North Eastern Railway's (LNER) William Teasdale. He and artist Norman Wilkinson, who suggested that the London Midland & Scotland Railway commission Royal Academicians to design its posters, were largely responsible for the British railway poster renaissance.

Nonetheless, it was incontestable that most American carriers remained reluctant to follow the westerners' lead. Indicative of this was an April 1925 Bureau of Railway Economics display of some four hundred travel posters in Washington, D.C.; not one was American, albeit thirteen were produced by the Canadian Pacific Railway. Finally, two long years later, the trade journal *Railway Age* was able to report some progress: "On several occasions we have called attention to, and reproduced, striking posters issued by the British railways. Perhaps no other industry anywhere has carried the advertising poster to such a high degree of artistic finish combined with advertising appeal." In fact, the editors were introducing a report on the B&O's progressive poster designs. By 1925, Chicago's Rapid Transit and interurban lines, New Haven, and New York Central had begun to experiment with posters. Northern Pacific, Illinois Central, Baltimore & Ohio, and Pennsylvania followed by decade's end.[4]

Santa Fe and Sam Hyde Harris

When railroad advertising was again permitted in 1920, Santa Fe promptly took up the reins, hiring Los Angeles commercial artist Sam Hyde Harris (1889–1977) to continue its poster work. For the most part, Harris created colorful, beautifully balanced renditions of romantic Southwest scenes that followed Treviso's and Bryn's idiom. His posters of the line's emblematic Navajo weaver and Grand Canyon offer color perspectives of how Treviso's originals might have appeared (figs. 61, 62). Others also borrowed subjects from the prewar years. One featured Bryn's rendering of the Chicago skyline, another incorporated the AT&SF logo into a Navajo blanket, a device first used in calendar designs (figs. 63, 64). Harris's own style is evident in 1925's "California Limited—

Fig. 61. (FACING PAGE) Sam Hyde Harris, 1924. George Theofiles, Miscellaneous Man.

Fig. 62. (RIGHT) Sam Hyde Harris, original artwork, tempera on board, ca. 1924. International Wildlife Commission, National Mustang Association.

A Transportation Triumph," which used brilliant red, blue, and yellow highlights to dramatize the figure of an Indian flute player. The design was so successful that the line reproduced it on the train's booklet covers and in newspaper ads; it was one of a handful of railroad productions published in *The Modern Poster Annual* (fig. 65).[5] All in all, Harris's posters showed that AT&SF management valued a consistent advertising image and message over artistic freedom.

Harris, an English immigrant, moved with his family to Los Angeles in 1904, at age fifteen. Although no record survives of how he met the railroad men, a few clues remain. During the 1910s, he studied with Hanson Putthoff, who painted background landscapes for Santa Fe exhibits; when he opened his own commercial studio on South Spring Street, it was only a few blocks away from Treviso's. Harris also designed for other lines, most often UP and SP, generally following the "Back East" theme. A contemporary maquette intended to promote SP's *Sunset Limited* provides an example of his talent for strong composition and subtle color. It focused on California's signature eucalyptus groves (fig. 66). Unfortunately, a much inferior design featuring the pervasive sunset motif was produced instead. On weekends and holidays Harris pursued his avocation, easel painting *en plein air;* in time he became known for his southwestern landscapes.

Southern Pacific and Maurice Logan

Southern Pacific's poster tradition was well established; indeed the line's consistent poster production disproved the oft-heard criticism that American railroads neglected the poster medium. The SP's creative message may not have been as focused as that of competitor AT&SF, but during the 1910s SP allocated more money than any other line to poster and large format advertising, making it second only to newspaper. The new emphasis also prompted the implementation of a standardized format: Posters were now printed in a unique quarter-sheet size, allowing the display of multiple images on station and ticket office notice boards. But through it all, noted one executive, the line's objective remained unchanged: "to people the empire of the West." To that end it continued to promote a full range of tourist destinations—beaches, lakes, and national parks; and the comfort of the limiteds that served them.

The number of artists SP employed and the diverse range of images that it produced attests to the breadth of its marketing effort. Californian Randal Borough (1878–1951) worked for SP during the 1910s, designing posters and booklets and illustrating for *Sunset* magazine. His images of western game—bears, rainbow trout—targeted sportsmen and evoked a romantic frontier appeal (fig. 67). Another noteworthy Borough design, the *Netherlands Route,* illustrated a second important promotional focus, agricultural development (fig. 68). Maynard Dixon contributed figurative variations on his famous *Sunset* magazine Indian poster of 1903, which saw use as booklet, poster, and billboard displays

Figs. 63 & 64. (ABOVE AND FACING PAGE) Sam Hyde Harris, original artwork, tempera on board, ca. 1924. International Wildlife Commission, National Mustang Association.

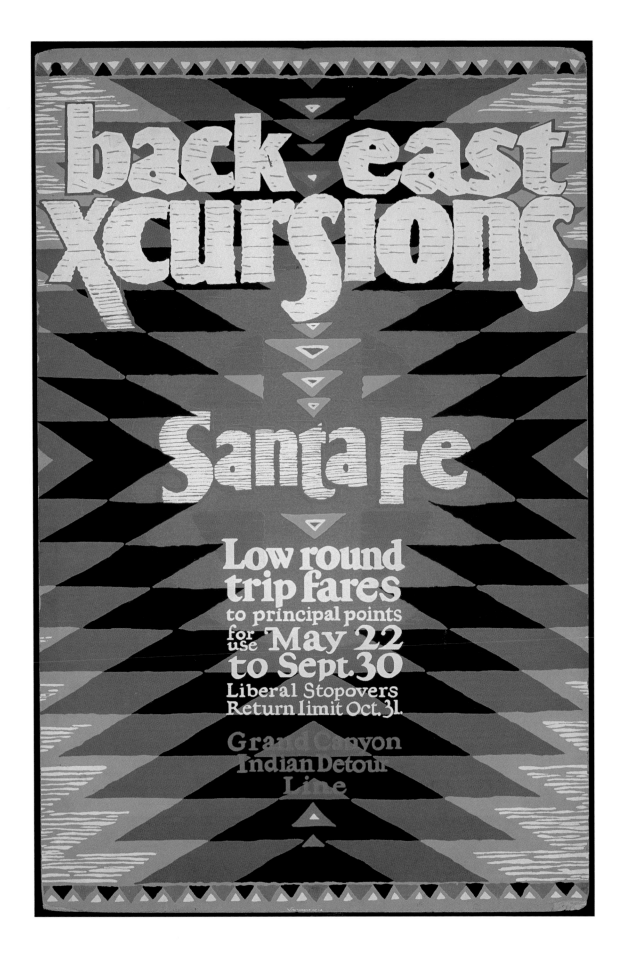

for the Apache Trail of 1918, a scenic side trip through Arizona's Salt River Valley made possible by the construction of Roosevelt Dam. Other car cards and posters designed by artists forgotten long ago sold Spanish Mission–styled resorts such as Paso Robles Hot Springs, the *Sunset Limited,* even a "Butterfly Trip" through the Berkeley and Alameda hills (figs. 69, 70, 71).

During the years immediately following World War I, SP continued to employ a broad range of both artists and themes. Sam Hyde Harris designed California mission scenes and placed golfers at the line's famed Hotel Del Monte. SP even produced an early skiing poster, 1922's *Winter Sports,* by Metcalf Morse. Other examples drew on prewar imagery: In

Fig. 65. (FACING PAGE) Sam Hyde Harris, 1925. International Wildlife Coalition, National Mustang Association.

Fig. 66. (ABOVE) Sam Hyde Harris, maquette for *Sunset Limited* poster, ca. 1924. International Wildlife Coalition, National Mustang Association.

Fig. 67. (RIGHT) Randal Borough, 1911, 20" x 32". California State Railroad Museum.

Fig. 68. (LEFT) Randal Borough, 1911, 18" x 32". California State Railroad Museum.

Figs. 69 & 70. (FACING PAGE TOP LEFT) Double car cards, 1912. New York Public Library.

Fig. 71. (FACING PAGE BOTTOM LEFT) Single sheet, 1912. New York Public Library.

Fig. 72. (FACING PAGE BOTTOM RIGHT) W. H. Bull, 1923, 16" x 23". Swann Galleries.

Bull's updated *Famed the World Round,* the *Sunset Limited* now flew across a vividly enhanced sunset sky, pulled by a modernized locomotive (fig. 72).

As the twenties progressed, SP management gradually came to the realization that their line's advertising would be more effective if it focused on a single memorable theme. Late in 1922, the line consolidated its advertising, placing it for the first time under the direction of a single agency, Lord & Thomas of San Francisco. While the campaign's longtime objective remained unaltered, its visuals changed dramatically, now focusing on California's romantic appeal. One of Lord & Thomas's most auspicious early actions was to commission San Francisco com-

mercial artist Maurice George Logan (1886–1977) to design a series of posters. Logan's productions were so well received that he designed for the line for more than a decade, creating a distinctive body of work that came to identify SP in the public mind. Indeed, SP would display his designs well into the era of streamlining.

A native of northern California, Logan recalled that he had always wanted to be an artist. He began taking art lessons at age twelve and attended art school in San Francisco for many years; he often quipped that he never stopped studying. His first commercial break came in 1912 in Chicago, where he studied at the Art Institute and worked with C. Everett Johnson, then Oscar Binner's head artist. By 1915 he had

Fig. 73. (LEFT) Southern Pacific bulletin-board poster display, ca. 1925. Union Pacific Historical Collection.

Fig. 74. (ABOVE) Maurice Logan portrait, 1922, by Louis Treviso. New York Public Library.

Fig. 75. (FACING PAGE) Maurice Logan, 1923, 16" x 23". Swann Galleries.

opened a commercial studio in San Francisco; by 1922 he had established himself as one of the West Coast's leading commercial artists and had begun to gain national recognition (fig. 74).

Logan's first SP posters, produced in 1923, found their roots in the same evolving "Western" school pioneered by Treviso and Bryn. Like them, he used the flat color effects of the German poster technique, painting with bold colors and relying on color contrast for depth. The series depicted women in emblematic settings: on a Pacific Ocean beach, dominated by sunshine and blue sky; riding a mule, in front of Half Dome's iconic profile; against Lake Tahoe's cerulean blue waters. He framed Tahoe with dark pine tree trunks and limbs reminiscent of Treviso's Grand Canyon designs. *Western Advertising* termed the series "rugged, almost, in technique" (figs. 75, 76, 77).[6]

Shortly after his SP assignment, Logan traveled to British East Africa, to sketch in preparation for a 1924 Los Angeles Museum of History, Science and Art commission to paint dioramas of African animals. He returned with a more vivid sense of color, which soon affected his style. The change made itself evident in brightly hued landscapes for a steadily lengthening list of clients, including Canadian Pacific, Standard Oil, and Matson Steamship Lines. Yet, as his commercial business prospered, he made time to pursue fine art, becoming a member of the Society of Six, a group of artists who painted outdoors on weekends. He became known for brilliantly colored, almost impressionistic, landscapes of characteristic California scenes—rounded hills, boat-filled harbors.

As his fine art increasingly influenced his commercial work, Logan pointed out that, if anything, the commercial work was the more demanding of the two: "Here's the distinction," he explained, "a poster is designed and a painting is not. . . . The commercial artist must think of his product and his message. He never loses himself in his work. He organizes his design." Logan's work was built around values, by which he meant "the relationship of colors to one another rather than rendering 'actual' colors." The title of a 1931 interview best summed up his approach: "A student paints what he sees, an artist paints what he knows." Partner Paul Carey concurred, recalling that a second Logan stylistic imperative was to simplify: "No matter what the subject, he simplified . . . both subject and manner."[7]

Figs. 76 & 77. (LEFT AND FACING PAGE) Maurice Logan, 1923, 16" x 23". Swann Galleries.

LAKE TAHOE

SOUTHERN PACIFIC

When in 1927 SP introduced a new promotional theme under the rubric "Four Great Routes," it again commissioned Logan to design the posters.[8] For this second series Logan drew landscapes typical of each route, this time including a train in many of his designs. A particularly vivid image—two *Overland Limited*s passing as they cross the Great Salt Lake in opposite directions—summed up the campaign and the era: It set a distinguished grouping upon the *Overland*'s observation platform, absorbed in the drama of both the West and western railroading (fig. 78).

The line so grew to admire his style that in 1928 it was made the campaign's focus. The man behind this melding of identities was general advertising agent K. C. Ingram, who in 1926–27, in concert with SP's agency, finally brought focus and direction to its disjointed advertising program. Ingram, a Bakersfield, California newspaperman who

worked in several promotional capacities, spearheaded the drive for a more consistent, readily recognizable public image. Late in 1926 his point of view prevailed as SP approved the "Four Great Routes" campaign.

Like his predecessor McCormick, Ingram used posters to build popular interest in western destinations. But now he refined the strategy, choosing to maximize campaign identity by presenting a uniform style. "Our posters have been standardized, chiefly through use of the work of the artist, Maurice Logan, and his style has been closely related to that used in our booklets and other advertising," Ingram reported to management in September 1928. Artwork now became a collaborative effort. San Francisco artist Fred Ludekens created the designs for booklets, magazines, and newspapers, while Logan painted destination posters. Ingram (further) standardized the campaign's graphics by using a consistent poster illustration size (quarter page), "clear-cut, easily-read typography," and white background border. Logan's work was so well received that it was gradually expanded to the other mediums. Ingram now made Logan's distinctive modern style synonymous with the SP name; like the sunset emblem itself, a readily recognized brand. His strategy proved an effective counter to the visual consistency exhibited by competitor AT&SF's Indian imagery.

As the campaign progressed, Logan's style also evolved. Concurrently, SP gave him free rein in both his poster style and selection of subjects. There was an intermediary between Logan and the SP, remembered associate Carey, "a one-man ad agency used to get Maury the paintings." This was likely H. A. Stebbins, publisher of *Western Advertising*. Logan's palette increasingly emphasized the brilliant colors emblematic of the California landscape—"backgrounds of purple summits, sapphire waters." He made increasing use of the impasto technique, applying heavy, textured swirls and strokes of oil paint to achieve depth and contrast. In his poster series of 1929–31, he cast Yosemite's iconic Half Dome in shades of blue and purple; New Orleans's wrought-iron railings recede into heavy brown-black shadows; and a diminutive train is nearly lost as it winds through the towering burnt orange mountains of remote Carriso Gorge, near the Mexican border east of San Diego (figs. 79, 80).

"Posters," Logan declared, "should give broad impressions rather than details, and yet the picture should depict the scene unmistakably. Commercial art is following fine art just as it has always done. When technique called for a network of details, commercial art was detailed, but with the modernistic tendencies of today, the simplicity characterizing fine art is carried into the commercial field. The old academician may continue to make anatomically perfect figures, but it is the modernistic art that gains public favor, and, after all, that is what the artist desires."[9]

Carey remembers that Logan kept largely to himself, that "he was a brilliant technician but not particularly articulate." Surprisingly, among

BY RAIL ACROSS
GREAT SALT LAKE
OVERLAND ROUTE

Southern Pacific

his greatest fans was Louis Treviso, who had selected his work for *Western Advertising*'s first "art cover" in 1921, and many more afterwards. Perhaps one artist best summed up another's talent. "The playful sunshine of his colors" and "his balanced rhythm in composition" were the qualities Treviso most admired.[10] Both were certainly evident in the images he created for SP.

Back East: The New Haven Begins

Ironically, the staid New Haven, a railroad that held a virtual monopoly on New England rail traffic and was famously disinclined to advertise, ventured into the poster club early on. The auto's inroads were first felt in resort traffic to the Adirondacks and New England. In response, NH was among the first lines to employ the inter-modal competitive sales appeal, "Travel by Train."

In 1924 the line commissioned New York City artist John Held, Jr., to design a series of posters selling New England resorts and vacations: Nantucket, Martha's Vineyard, the Berkshires. Held, a well-known delineator of eastern establishment culture whose *Vanity Fair* and *Life* magazine illustrations and cartoons introduced two of the era's defining caricatures—the happy-go-lucky flapper and her straw-hatted guy, Joe College—proved a prescient choice. His New Haven designs talked to the new, jazzy cultural elite; indeed, the line hired him before even *The New Yorker* magazine!

Held's first poster, *From Pines to Palms via the Hell Gate Bridge Route* (Nov. 1, 1924), was driven more by advertising formula than any particular artistic style—it simply pictured characteristic scenes, north and south, linked together by the famous bridge. Fortunately, client NH quickly realized the value of Held's trademark moon-faced cartoon characters, and they were made the prominent feature of *Nantucket* (Jan. 1, 1925); of course, they proved a hit. Held started out as an advertising artist for Colliers Street Railway Advertising Co., designing car cards for John Wanamaker. Friend and art historian Weinhardt observed that he "was extraordinarily sensitive to color." Held became known for "his outrageous combinations of violent hues," of which *Northward!* is a fine example (figs. 81, 82).

New York Central's Art Posters

Central management stated that their poster campaign drew its inspiration from the success of the poster idea abroad, especially in England. Central produced what it termed art posters, employing the appeal of place, untainted by even the slightest suggestion of commercialism. Central's interest in posters evolved gradually, drawing its roots from a formidable promotional heritage and a successful calendar program begun in 1922.

Central's reputation as railroading's most effective advertiser had

Fig. 78. (FACING PAGE) Maurice Logan, 1927, 16" x 23".

Fig. 79. (ABOVE) Maurice Logan, 1929, 16" x 23".

Fig. 80. Maurice Logan, 1929, 16" x 23".

Fig. 81. John Held, Jr., ca. 1930. Swann Galleries.

Fig. 82. John Held's *The Enchanted Isle*, 1934, followed style of earlier *Nantucket*. Swann Galleries.

been forged by George H. Daniels, whose tenets were consistency of message and its pervasive application. Daniels well understood the selling power of an iconic image. Throughout the 1890s he had blanketed the nation with images of Central's world record–breaking speedster, the *Empire State Express*. In 1902 he coined the name *20th Century Limited* and built a similar campaign with the objective of making it the most famous train in the world.

A decade later, Daniels's successors made good on his claim.[11] The *Century*'s success was attributable to a combination of effective advertising and management attention, from president A. H. Smith on down through the ranks. Its advertising campaign made frequent use of the image of a speeding train, drawn by George Ethridge, a pioneer in applying the poster's eye-catching simplicity to advertising art. In time, even the image became an icon. When in 1917 Smith commissioned editor and artist William Harnden Foster (1886–1941), best known for rendering racing automobiles, to paint a picture of the *Century* at speed, the completed image bore a remarkable resemblance to Ethridge's design. Titled *The 20th Century Limited—The Greatest Train in the World*, the painting became the symbol of both train and railroad (fig. 83).

After the war, traffic vice-president George H. Ingalls directed NYC's ad agency, Thomas F. Logan, Inc., to recast the image for a new calendar campaign. Ingalls's stated marketing objective was to promote the idea of the *20th Century*'s speed by using "Art," in the expectation that an artistic image might increase the calendar's display value and, thus, its utility. The experiment proved a huge success: For the first year of 1922 they produced fifty thousand; the following year twice as many were called for. Ingalls reported that patrons and shippers, particularly on-line businesses and banks, framed the calendar images for display in offices and boardrooms (fig. 84).

Ingalls began Central's poster campaign in 1925, in concert with planning the line's centennial celebration. Driven more by marketing strategy than allegiance to any particular artistic style, Central's effort initially focused on the rich historical lore of its Hudson River Valley route and the machinery of the nation's industrial heartland, a great deal of which it and its predecessor lines had helped develop. Ingalls also headed up the committee which chose subjects and commissioned artists, selecting them for their characteristic style and permitting them free rein in the handling of their subject.

As had LNER's advertising manager William Teasdale, Central's "advertising counsel" Frank H. Fayant commissioned works by a range of prominent commercial artists. He further followed Teasdale's objective: producing pictures "designed as an advertisement—to catch the eye— the imagination—the pocket—of people of all kinds." Still, in keeping with American taste, Central's posters were essentially landscape paintings reproduced in chromolithography, wrapped in elegantly detailed borders. But for a few exceptions, they had little in common with the "bold, simplified views carried out in flat colors with an elimination of

The Century—
the world's most famous train

The Twentieth Century Limited, when it inaugurated the 20-hour service between New York and Chicago, brought the two greatest markets of the country within overnight reach of each other. This saving of a business day has been of incalculable value to industry, commerce and finance.

With ceaseless regularity this world-famous train—for more than 7,000 nights—has been making its scheduled flight between the port of New York and the head of Lake Michigan over *the water level route* of the New York Central Lines.

Travelers whose business takes them frequently back and forth between Chicago and New York

habitually use the "Century" because of its deserved reputation as the most comfortable long-distance, fast train in the world.

The equipment of the "Century" is maintained at the highest standard; its appointments, conveniences and cuisine are planned to meet the desires of the most exacting travelers; it lands its passengers in the heart of Chicago and New York.

The Twentieth Century Limited is the pride of the employees who operate it and guard it night after night, and it is the standard bearer of a service known the world over as the highest development of railroad transportation.

New York - Chicago
20-hour service

"Century" Westbound
New York 2.45 p.m.
Chicago 9.45 a.m.

"Century" Eastbound
Chicago 12.40 p.m.
New York 9.40 a.m.

NEW YORK CENTRAL LINES

BOSTON & ALBANY – MICHIGAN CENTRAL – BIG FOUR – LAKE ERIE & WESTERN
KANAWHA & MICHIGAN – TOLEDO & OHIO CENTRAL – PITTSBURGH & LAKE ERIE
NEW YORK CENTRAL · AND · SUBSIDIARY LINES

Fig. 83. (TOP) William H. Foster's 1917 *20th Century Limited* painting, also used to illustrate New York Central's first calendar, 1922.

Fig. 84. (BOTTOM) Herbert M. Stoops, "speeding *Century*" artwork, 1921.

unnecessary details," at which contemporary British artists, particularly Tom Purvis and Norman Wilkinson, were famously adept.[12]

Central's first poster (July 1925) commemorated the commissioning of its massive high-level Hudson River bridge at Castleton, New York (fig. 85). Herbert Morton Stoops (1887–1948), a New York artist best known for his wartime art and western scenes, chose to focus his work on the bulk of the span's soaring concrete piers, atop which a locomotive's steam trail is just barely visible. Artist Stoops's subject and massing recall several contemporary British LNER posters by Royal Academician Frank Brangwyn, particularly *The Royal Border Bridge, Scotland,* produced earlier that same year. In October 1926, Stoops continued the industrial theme, rendering the great hulking cranes at Ashtabula Harbor, "where trainloads of Appalachian coal are exchanged for cargoes of Northern iron ore" (fig. 86). (A second example is Brangwyn's high-level bridge at Newcastle on Thyn.)

Central produced its second poster nearly a year later, in July 1926. Jon O. Brubaker's *California, America's Vacation Land,* a powerfully evocative depiction of California's distinctive golden hills aglow in sunset hues, sold "western wanderlust" (fig. 87). Brubaker (1875–?), whom Central's publicists termed "one of the foremost poster artists of the country," was well known for his "color harmony and tone quality." A California resident who was best known for his interpretation of California subjects, his work was often included in the New York Art Directors Club's annual exhibition. *California* proved to be the most popular and remunerative of the series, setting the campaign's success; other executions followed in quick succession.[13]

Adolph Treidler, arguably the nation's most outstanding poster artist, was another obvious choice. Central produced his *New York, The Wonder City of the World* in January 1927 (fig. 88). Fifty years later, Treidler recalled his Liberty Loan poster of 1918 and this "night view of lower Manhattan with the Statue of Liberty large in the foreground" as his two best-known works. An outspoken practitioner and advocate of the European poster technique, he used flat color effects, rather than light and shade, in setting his values. Treidler ascribed the American public's attachment to detailed illustration to clients and ad men who underestimated their ability to appreciate good design. Nevertheless, NYC agency Lord & Thomas and Logan paired his image with the matchless "Wonder City" copyline.[14] Both Stoops's and Treidler's work were included in the prestigious annual exhibitions of the New York Art Directors Club.

Earl Horter's March 1927 etching of Grand Central Terminal's main concourse revealed a Modernist influence (fig. 89). Horter filled the renowned mixing space with sketchily abstract figures, making it pulse with energy as bands of sepia-toned light gave depth to the vast expanse beneath the barrel-vaulted ceiling. Horter (1883–1940), one of the country's distinguished etchers, had worked as an advertising artist for Phoebe Snow creator E. E. Calkins, while studying and drawing at night

school. And again, Central's agency provided first-rate copy, naming the terminal "The Gateway to a Continent."

To be fair, other artists designed more typical posters. Frank Hazell contributed a traditional autumn view of the United States Military Academy at West Point (fig. 90). Fredrick Madan painted Niagara Falls; Anthony Hansen, Hudson Valley and New England landscapes; Robert O. Reid, the Hudson Highlands. Walter Greene, a staff artist for General Electric who specialized in formulaic calendar depictions of locomotives and ships, and who also painted five of the Central's famous annual calendar scenes, designed posters of the Hudson River Highlands and Adirondacks (fig. 91). Unfortunately, Russell Patterson, creator of the twenties' emblematic flapper and designer of tens of stylish newspaper drawings of prosperous, self-assured patrons boarding the *20th Century* at Grand Central, contributed only one, an altogether unremarkable painting of the Mohawk Valley.[15]

Central showed its considerable promotional mettle in winning broad distribution and display of its posters. In addition to the usual station notice boards and downtown display windows, Central installed special display areas in its big-city terminals and maintained broad reach overseas; its sales agent, American Express Co., displayed the posters from Cairo to Stockholm. A 1928 halftone shows both Treidler's *Wonder City* and Horter's *Grand Central* on display beside several Cunard Lines posters at the Egyptian State Railway's Cairo terminal. Beginning in autumn 1926, Central further reinforced the posters' impact by featuring black-and-white versions in its national magazine advertising campaign, which ran in high circulation weeklies such as the *Saturday Evening Post, Time,* and *Literary Digest.* Central's example confirmed that the roads that went to the trouble to produce effective posters (Central, Santa Fe, and SP) used them to full advantage.

Chesley Bonestell (1888–1986), the designer of a poster produced in February 1930 spotlighting the new New York Central Building astride Park Avenue, was one of the nation's foremost architectural artists (fig. 92). Well versed on trends in modern design, Bonestell had worked with architects Cass Gilbert and William Van Allen, for whom he designed the ceiling murals and elevator car finish for New York City's Chrysler Building. At the time of his commission, he was employed by Warren & Wetmore, the subject's architects. As had Treidler, he used the powerful device of spotlights and nighttime illumination to dramatize the building's unique setting.

In an interview, Bonestell offered a perspective on the twin objectives of creating an eye-catching image while also accommodating the American preference for realism:

> Contrary to the usual conception, I see no objection to detail provided it does not weaken or confuse the design. There has long been a theory that much should be left to the imagination, and posters should be just masses. Since posters are intended to promote business

Fig. 85. Herbert M. Stoops, July 1925.

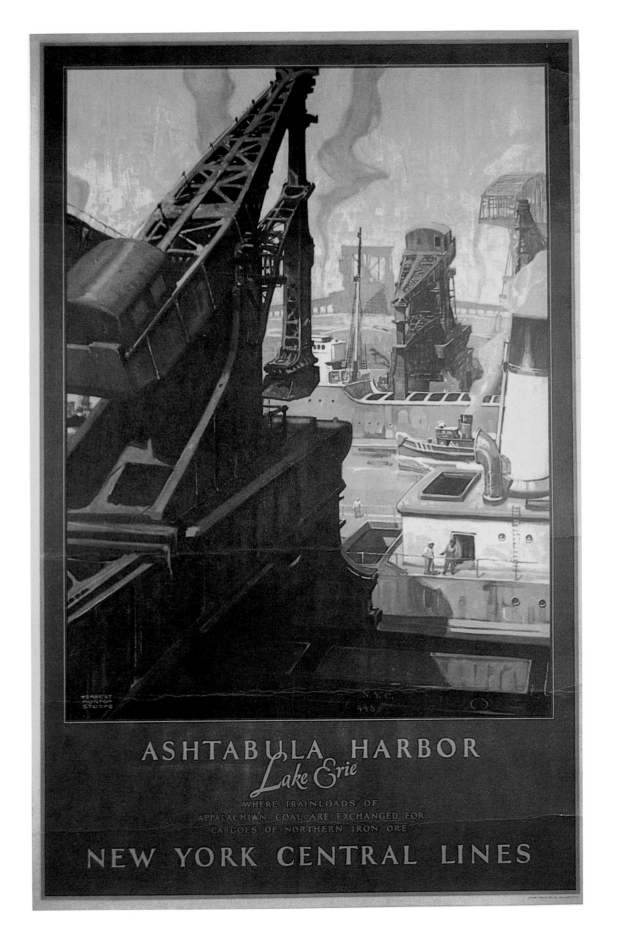

Fig. 86. Herbert M. Stoops, October 1926.

Fig. 87. Jon Brubaker, July 1926.
PosterConnection, Inc.

Fig. 88. Adolph Treidler, January 1927.

Fig. 89. Earl Horter, March 1927.

WEST POINT
UNITED STATES MILITARY ACADEMY
In the Highlands of the Hudson
NEW YORK CENTRAL LINES

STORM KING
IN THE HEART OF THE HUDSON HIGHLANDS
NEW YORK CENTRAL LINES

and the average businessman has no imagination, it is well to put in detail where possible without detracting from the power of the general design.

The public are always delighted with detail, apparently curious as to how the artist interprets it and, if possible, discover mistakes, and as posters are a commercial proposition it is important to please the public.[16]

Upon his return to the Central in April 1929, after an absence of eight years, longtime ad manager P. V. D. Lockwood awarded a commission to a Chicago artist who had just moved east with his new bride. Leslie Ragan's first NYC poster appeared in January 1930 (see chap. 5).

Hernando G. Villa and the Santa Fe *Chief*

Finding Hernando Villa is an example of how a wide-ranging corporate interest in southwestern history and art characterized Santa Fe management. While his images were determinedly rooted in the AT&SF tradition of portrait and landscape painting from which Treviso and Bryn had sought to break, they nevertheless exhibited the same overriding attributes—focused design and bold use of color. Villa's Santa Fe poster designs struck such a popular chord that they both dominated and inspired the line's advertising output until it exited the passenger-carrying business in 1971 (fig. 93).

Fig. 90. (FACING PAGE LEFT) Frank Hazell, 1927. Swann Galleries.

Fig. 91. (FACING PAGE RIGHT) Walter Greene, 1928. Swann Galleries.

Fig. 92. (RIGHT) Chesley Bonestell, February 1930.

NEW YORK CENTRAL BUILDING

PARK AVENUE, NEW YORK

AT · THE · GATEWAY · TO · A · CONTINENT

Writing in 1929, Los Angeles art critic Prudence Woolett observed that the Santa Fe had brought poster design to a higher state of perfection than any other American business organization.[17] While Woolett's immediate subject was a series of posters by Hernando Villa, she credited the company with more than fifteen years of "us[ing] the colored poster in its purest form" to stimulate interest in its territory. What distinguished the Santa Fe? It possessed no unique natural advantage among western railroads—every one of which offered an abundance of wonders. Ironically, SP's K. C. Ingram, the man who set advertising strategy for the competition, said it best: "Uniformity of style, centralization of control and continuity of theme are the fundamentals of all good advertising," he wrote to his management in a memo that framed potential responses to the Santa Fe's campaign.[18] Among the western lines, only AT&SF consistently applied all three.

The circumstance of Villa's association with the Santa Fe is shrouded in myth. He appeared on the scene in 1928, two years after the Santa Fe had inaugurated the *Chief,* a deluxe limited that inspired its own set of legends. His work and *The Chief* name are inextricably commingled.

The Santa Fe *Chief* was brought into being as the southern California boom reignited in the go-go twenties, providing a strong growth trend in transcontinental Pullman traffic for Santa Fe and competitor SP. As the decade progressed, the business community began to press for a quickening of the best Chicago–California running time, then a lethargic seventy-two hours. Both circumstances prompted increased service and the establishment of a sixty-three-hour Chicago to Los Angeles schedule late in 1926.

C. J. Birchfield, now second in command of the AT&SF advertising department, coined the new flyer's name. According to *Advertising Age,* his choice "was attuned to the Indian saga characteristic of the company's advertising."[19] Birchfield's colleagues thought the name inspired, as it embodied both Santa Fe's traditional southwestern theme and its long-established market primacy.

The train's distinctive logo, a profile of a warbonnet-clad Indian chief's head set against a Santa Fe cross logo on the diagonal, recalled Louis Treviso's prewar work. First used as the observation car drumhead, the design soon graced nearly every AT&SF ad. The search for an equally distinctive advertising campaign proved more challenging. Early ads for the train, designed by leading western artists, featured a range of Indian chief images, each attired in the emblematic warbonnet; however, none proved sufficiently vivid. Longtime Fred Harvey Company artist Fred Geary drew the first, a head-on portrait; Arizonan Lon Megargee contributed an elderly chief gazing at migrating geese.

AT&SF myth has it that Villa was discovered in 1928 by Los Angeles ad manager H. D. Dodge who attended an exhibition of Villa's paintings at the suggestion of an associate. "See what you can do in the way of giving us an Indian to symbolize our train, 'The Chief,'" an impressed

Dodge is said to have requested after the visit. "It didn't prove easy," recalled Villa. "I handed in a sketch of an old wrinkled Indian but it wasn't accepted. They wanted a man in his prime—an Indian of dignity and poise." Villa returned to his easel and created the definitive *Chief* icon, all head, shoulders, and warbonnet: an image that inspired both dreams of adventure and a shudder of fear (figs. 94, 95).[20]

In fact, Villa's association with the Santa Fe dates to 1905, when he was still an art school student. During those early years he designed ads for the Santa Fe's Los Angeles office, along with the SP and the Los Angeles & Salt Lake. His early illustrations showed an Arts and Crafts influence, setting elegant women on observation car platforms and limiteds charging out of California poppies. There was something lyrical about the way in which Villa's landscapes unwound, looking out from the rear of a train: where he set a mission church, how he posed a señorita.

Of Castilian descent, Villa (1881–1952) kept a studio in Los

Angeles's historic Alameda district, where his family had lived for generations. His father had studied art when Los Angeles was still more pueblo than boomtown; his mother was an accomplished musician who sang and played for Charles F. Lummis's landmark recordings of early Spanish California songs. He was fascinated by Native Americans from youth: "Before drawing a line I spent six months with the Arapahoes, studying them and learning their ways." In the tradition of Burbank, Louis Akin, and Sauerwein, he made the pilgrimage to the ancient pueblos of Taos and Acoma to study and live the traditional life as artists had done for generations. Villa treated Native Americans with a respect that approached reverence and sought to dispel the stereotypical attitude that they all looked alike. He expressed hope that his images would contribute to a more enlightened outlook. "You must have a feeling for the Indian to portray him," he declared. "Nobody can tell you how to draw him and you cannot learn it from books. Not only must there be a knowledge of the anatomy and customs, but there must be a love for the

Fig. 93. (FACING PAGE) Hernando G. Villa in his Los Angeles studio, ca. 1930.

Fig. 94. (LEFT) Hernando Villa, 1929. New York Public Library.

Fig. 95. (ABOVE) Hernando Villa's Chief reproduced as a magazine ad, 1929.

Fig. 96. (LEFT) Hernando Villa's "perfected Chief," 1930, reproduced as a magazine ad.

Fig. 97. (FACING PAGE TOP) Hernando Villa, 1930, reproduced as a magazine ad.

Fig. 98. (FACING PAGE BOTTOM) Hernando Villa, 1929.

Indian." To Villa, the Chief represented "an ideal Indian, ... typifying the handsome Navajo," Dodge observed.[21] Villa himself recalled that it took him three years to perfect the *Chief* symbol (fig. 96).

As Villa's Chief came to signify Santa Fe service, his range of poster subjects expanded to include the Grand Canyon, Indian pueblos and ceremonies, the line's "Indian-detour" side trips, and California's Spanish fiestas. Like his Chief profiles, these images were carefully designed, using composition and color to make a strong impression. Taos Indians gather around a drummer before the famed pueblo (fig. 97). Towering thunderheads and a lone horseman lend a feeling of solitude to *In the Indian-detour Country;* the pueblo in the distance recalls a description the line's pioneering ad man C. A. Higgins penned in 1892: "fair white castles cresting the cliffs of a desert waste" (fig. 98). Still, his work represents a definite change in style from the flat colors, simplified images, and looming logos of the Treviso years. Ironically, with Villa's artwork the AT&SF's appropriation of the image of the Native American was now complete: The Chief himself had been made to represent the Santa Fe, and the line's logo thereby greatly diminished in prominence (fig. 99).

Villa's Chief portraits became immensely popular, so much so that the series soon played a determining role in the overall campaign, even the famous Indian calendar series, illustrated by Taos, New Mexico artist Eanger Irving Couse. "Am enclosing samples of our use of the Chief head in recent posters and advertisements," W. H. Simpson wrote Couse in the process of developing the 1932 calendar. "Our calendar picture, while being different from the Hernando Villa heads, should in a way suggest them, especially as to the war bonnet and the profile."[22] In order to heighten popular interest in the Chief campaign, the line changed images two or three times a year and adapted them, greatly simplified, to California billboard displays. In the process the Chief grew increasingly stylized and his designs acquired an Art Deco motif: patterned backgrounds replaced solids, "moderne" displaced hand lettering, colors grew increasingly saturated, and the profiles took on a supernatural quality.

True to form, Simpson again treated the artwork as he did fine art, framing the originals for display, waiting until 1931 to reproduce them as posters. Simpson's window displays of the 1930s show an alluring blend of art and posters; he shrewdly used the Southwest's romantic appeal in order to gain wide circulation by exchange with other railroads (fig. 100).

Throughout, Villa remained extraordinarily enthusiastic about his advertising work. Photographs show him posing in a chief's robes and warbonnet at the rim of the Grand Canyon. In one he strikes the very attitude of his first Chief portrait, even donning the model warbonnet (fig. 101). His posters of the early thirties ranged across every aspect of promotion: 1932's Los Angeles Olympics shows Indians racing; the 1933 Chicago World's Fair, a brave holding the city aloft. The campaign ran

Fig. 99. (LEFT) Hernando Villa, 1931.

Fig. 100. (FACING PAGE TOP) Hernando Villa's Santa Fe posters on display in Baltimore & Ohio Louisville, Kentucky ticket-office window, 1934. Kansas State Historical Society.

Fig. 101. (FACING PAGE BOTTOM) Hernando Villa at Grand Canyon, ca. 1930. Southwest Museum, Los Angeles. #43077.

through the mid-1930s to be replaced by streamlining's Art Deco–inspired Native American imagery. The old saw, "imitation is the best form of flattery," perhaps best sums up its resounding popularity: When in 1935 Transcontinental & Western Airlines, which followed the Santa Fe's route, introduced new Douglas aircraft, its four-color full-page magazine ads featured a "Sky Chief" symbol and moniker.

The Canadian Pacific and Others

To be sure, other lines produced posters during the decade of the 1920s. Canadian Pacific, among the most aggressive users of the medium, promoted a broad range of products—ships, resort hotels, and Rocky Mountain scenery—with posters. The most vivid of the series, by New York City artist W. Langdon Kihn, who was well known for his Indian drawings, sold Banff Indian Days, a summertime tourist festival (fig. 102). Also noteworthy was Will Hollingsworth's rendering in shades of summertime pastel of the famed Chateau Frontenac at Quebec City (fig. 103). When still an art student in Chicago in 1916, Hollingsworth won a competition prize with a railroad poster design promoting Yellowstone National Park.[23] CP publicity agent, C. W. Stokes, suggested that in order to be effective a poster must convey an idea, "to explode a bombshell under the consciousness." The best CP work did just that—it was arrestingly vivid.[24]

Considering its pioneering role in railroad promotion, Northern Pacific came late to the poster medium, waiting until the mid-1920s to produce images of Yellowstone National Park, the Pacific Northwest, and a dramatic series depicting its flyer, the *North Coast Limited*. Like its diverse subject matter, NP's imagery ran the gamut, ranging from pure poster designs to enlarged landscape paintings and cartoons.

The third transcontinental line, which NP opened in September 1883 (SP's Sunset Route opened February 1883), passed within forty miles of Yellowstone National Park and thus originated NP's "Wonderland" moniker. NP's longtime ad man Olin Dunbar Wheeler believed strongly in the booklet medium; for nearly two decades his annual "Wonderland" production was the centerpiece of the line's campaign. NP was also among the first lines to commission western art. "NP soon after its opening hired an artist to paint some of the characteristic scenes of its route and Mr. Keith was recommended," western boomer and historian Charles F. Lummis wrote in 1898, by way of introducing the leading painters of the Pacific Coast. Lummis termed William Keith the "American Turner," and the NP displayed his work across its system, albeit on a much more limited scale than AT&SF.[25] Wheeler also commissioned Joseph Chenoweth, known for his scenes of the Lewis and Clark Expedition, another cornerstone of NP promotion. Prominent commercial artists also contributed to NP's effort, notably J. C. Leyendecker and Alfred Lenz, who produced delicate landscapes modeled in plaster.

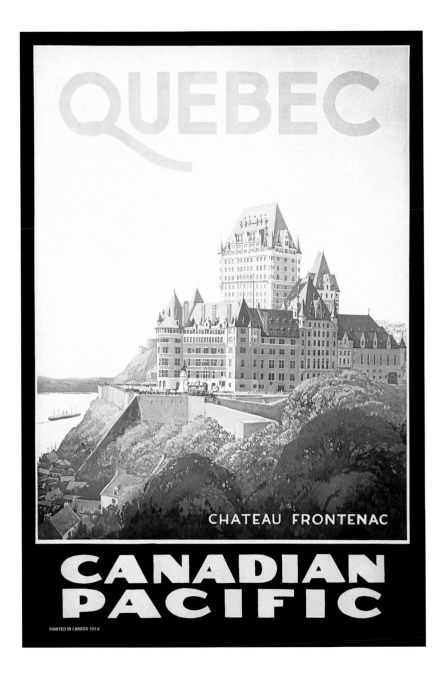

CHATEAU FRONTENAC

CANADIAN PACIFIC

PRINTED IN CANADA 1924

Fig. 102. (FACING PAGE) W. Langdon Kihn, ca. 1930.

Fig. 103. (ABOVE) Will Hollingsworth, 1924.

General passenger agent Max Goodsill introduced NP's poster series after Wheeler's retirement in 1923. Likely the first and certainly the most reproduced poster image was a lithograph of Thomas Moran's famous painting *Grand Canyon of the Yellowstone,* which NP's directors had a hand in creating back in 1872. The upgrading of the *North Coast Limited* in the spring of 1930 prompted the campaign's expansion, but the Depression's mounting losses assured that it was to be short-lived. Goodsill commissioned Minneapolis muralist and portrait painter Gustav Krollmann (1888–1962) to design the work. Born and trained in Vienna, Krollmann set the new train speeding through the Northwest landscape, in images that displayed a strong sense of modeling and a richness of color. The first and most often reproduced of the series, *North Coast Limited in the Montana Rockies,* employed a particularly dramatic perspective (fig. 104). The popular success of his series prompted Goodsill to expand the campaign (fig. 105).

Alaskan artist Sydney M. Laurence, who led the life of a Jack London adventure-story hero, created what were perhaps NP's most compelling images. Gold fever led him to Alaska in 1903, where he took up landscape painting after incurring injuries in a shipwreck. Goodsill acquired the rights to reproduce his paintings as posters and ads beginning in 1930. If more picture than poster, Laurence's luminous views of snow-capped peaks nevertheless conveyed a world of mystery and adventure (fig. 106). *Off to the Potlatch,* which set Northwest Indians in a traditional dugout canoe sailing to a festival of giving, proved most popular; its poster version won first prize in a contemporary Boston exhibition (fig. 107). Goodsill wanted nothing more than for him to paint a Yellowstone scene; however, Laurence demurred, saying he could not "paint smells."[26]

Goodsill also produced more typical western subjects. Edward P. Bremer painted *Yellowstone,* an impressionistic, spectral view of the Old Faithful Geyser, while his *Rodeo Parade* focused on a warbonneted Plains Indian. Cartoonist J. Hilton created risqué cartoons of dude ranching. But by the mid-thirties, NP had exited the poster business, although many images were subsequently reissued in the postwar years.

Great Northern, NP's companion line across the Northwest, produced an occasional billboard promoting its flagship *Oriental Limited;* however, it made little use of posters. Instead, GN was well known for calendars promoting Glacier National Park, illustrated with paintings of the region's Blackfeet Indians by noted artist Winold Reiss.

As noted in *Railway Age,* Baltimore & Ohio commissioned four posters to announce its centenary pageant in 1927. The most effective designs compared the line's first locomotive, tiny *Tom Thumb,* to the modern Pacific-class *President Washington.* George Illian's traditional broadside-inspired work won display at a New York Art Directors Club exhibition; L. Vasser Elam's artwork offset colonial buildings with skyscrapers, and proved to be most dramatic (fig. 108).

Illinois Central had occasionally used posters to promote its crack

Fig. 104. (ABOVE LEFT) Gustav Krollmann, 1929.

Fig. 105. (ABOVE RIGHT) Gustav Krollmann, 1930. Swann Galleries.

Fig. 106. (FACING PAGE TOP) Sydney Laurence, *Rainier—from Yakima,* 1932, reproduced as magazine ad.

Fig. 107. (FACING PAGE BOTTOM) Sydney Laurence, *Off to the Potlatch,* 1931, reproduced as magazine ad.

Florida train, *The Seminole,* since the late teens. A decade later, IC commissioned Chicago designer Paul Proehl (1887–1965) to create scenes of Chicago, which it dubbed America's "Vacation City," and Mississippi Gulf Coast resorts (fig. 109). Proehl had initially studied architecture and worked as a draftsman, but boredom prompted him to change careers; in 1918 he signed on as an advertising artist with the Chicago firm of Charles Daniel Frey. Behind the campaign was IC president Charles H. Markham, known for a progressive public relations outlook. He attributed his success to marketing "based on good service, straight talk and plenty of it."[27]

The Pennsylvania experimented with a broad range of large-format advertising throughout the twenties. Conservative and engineering-oriented, PRR management found itself in a perennial game of promotional catch-up with its more sophisticated rival NYC. Like Central, PRR started with calendars, beginning its series in 1925, two years after its nemesis (fig. 111). A suggestion by the Edward G. Budd Manufacturing Co. for securing a painting of the line's flagship *Broadway Limited* prompted the move. The idea caught the fancy of PRR president Samuel Rea, who told his staff: "I certainly would not advocate . . . a picture like the 20th Century, which is practically a picture of the locomotive—and head-on, at that. It seems to me that a view that would include the train and perhaps show the color of our Broadway Limited might be desirable."[28] To Rea's credit, the artists whom PRR commissioned to design its calendars did manage to distinguish the series from Central's by focusing on its distinctive Tuscan red passenger cars.

PRR began experimenting with posters in the mid-twenties, at first reformatting the most popular of its annual calendar paintings as single-sheet posters for European distribution. In 1927, in concert with the *Broadway Limited*'s twenty-fifth anniversary, the line also commissioned a winning set of urban billboards that featured special illumination and moving parts—revolving locomotive driving wheels, puffing steam, glowing headlights (fig. 112). Still, it was not until 1929 that PRR turned to posters in a big way, commissioning a series of six that were also designed for use as car cards. Their range of subjects—Pennsylvania Station in New York, the "Gateway to America"; Independence Hall; Horseshoe Curve; even a California view—again copied Central's strategy (fig. 113). All were designed by Ivar Gull, a New York City artist who, according to producer Charles Francis Press, "trained in the best European schools of modern design"; he also illustrated the line's timetables (fig. 114).

Like NP, PRR's most noteworthy campaign was cut short by the Depression. Late in 1929 Ivy Lee, the nation's prototypical public relations man, of whose services the PRR had availed itself back in 1912 for the princely annual salary of $10,000, hired its most prominent illustrator, N. C. Wyeth (1882–1945), to design a dozen posters of patriotic images. The campaign's objective was "to illustrate and emphasize the historical associations in which PRR territory is so rich." True to the

Mt. Rainier, at Sunrise, from a Painting by Sydney Laurence

 Rainier—from Yakima

A new entrance to Rainier National Park opens this summer— **The Yakima Gateway.** From Yakima, Wash., on the main line of the Northern Pacific to the Pacific Coast, guests are motored along a majestic avenue of orchards, rivers, canyons and forests to Sunrise Lodge—the most thrilling mountain trip imaginable.

For travel arrangements or use, from Rainier Bank, address E. E. Nelson, 512 Northern Pacific Bldg., St. Paul, Minn.

Traveling West? We invite you to use the custom-built, roller-bearing, no extra-fare—

NORTH COAST LIMITED • NEWEST OF TRANSCONTINENTAL TRAINS

"OFF IN THE FIORLAND"

N o r t h

As on a Dream Ship, one floats luxuriously to Alaska, mountains of heavenly beauty alongside. Planned cruises, recommended by the Northern Pacific Railway, include:

Upon request, this album free

Inside Passage	Gulf of Alaska	Mt. McKinley	Yukon River	7,000 Islands
$309.06	$382.26	$527.28	$625	$266.56

All expenses, round trip, from Chicago. Rates from other cities promptly given.

To the Pacific Northwest and Alaska, the New North Coast Limited Newest of Transcontinental Trains

For Alaska Album and information about Alaskan cruises, address E. E. Nelson, 345 Northern Pacific Ry., St. Paul, Minn.

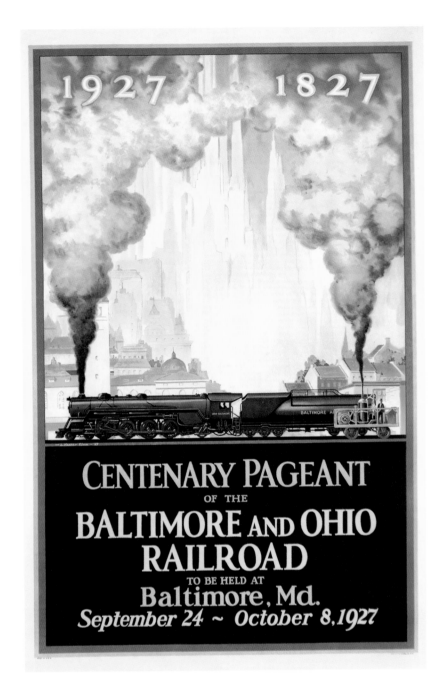

Fig. 108. (ABOVE LEFT) L. Vasser Elam, 1927. Swann Galleries.

Fig. 109. (FACING PAGE) Paul Proehl, ca. 1929.

Fig. 110. (ABOVE RIGHT) Oscar Rabe Hanson, 1926; representative of early Chicago interurban and transit poster advertising.

road's conservative outlook, Lee's correspondence made special note of the fact that he had considered "bringing some Englishman over," but instead, decided that an "American touch" would be essential for such a dignified commission. "I am convinced," he concluded, that "N. C. Wyeth is the outstanding poster painter of the country." Wyeth's characteristic sense of historical accuracy and dramatic composition made for a perfect fit. The first of the series, *Ringing Out Liberty,* debuted in May 1930. Ultimately, only four were produced (figs. 115, 116).[29]

Daytime and Night-time

GRAPHIC, colorful and realistic, this painted bulletin during daylight hours focuses the attention of thousands in Chicago on the famous *Broadway* train of the Pennsylvania Railroad. When night falls, an ingenious mechanical lighting system adds further interest. Wheels revolve—rails recede—smoke streams back—headlight gleams—periodic flares light up the cab as the fire box door is opened—and *The Broadway* speeds on thru the night. Similar bulletins in St. Louis, Detroit and other cities, feature other crack trains of the Pennsylvania System.

General Outdoor Advertising Co.

One Park Avenue
New York
Harrison & Loomis Sts.
Chicago
Sales Offices and Branches in 60 other Cities

Unfortunately, the posters received little public notice. Though Lee and PRR management possessed the foresight to secure an artist of national reputation, they remained remarkably naïve about gaining public display for their images. PRR limited distribution to schools and libraries, and, of course, its own stations and ticket offices. While uncertainty due to the Depression doubtless hindered the effort's potential, it appears to have been created in a vacuum. PRR's press release supports this, contending that before its initiative, "the development of the railroad poster has heretofore been on a comparatively limited scale." If anything, PRR's behavior reflected the characteristically self-centered—it preferred to use the term "standard"—way the line did practically everything.[30] Still, as the Depression eased, Pennsy returned to posters, producing images by calendar artist Grif Teller, and, most notably, those featuring Atlantic City and Washington, D.C. by Edward Eggleston (1883–1941).

Fig. 111. (ABOVE LEFT) Harold Brett's 1925 painting *Speed & Security* inaugurated Pennsylvania Railroad's calendar series.

Fig. 112. (ABOVE RIGHT) Billboard, Chicago, 1927.

Fig. 113. (FACING PAGE LEFT) Ivar Gull, 1929.

Fig. 114. (FACING PAGE RIGHT) Ivar Gull, car cards, 1929.

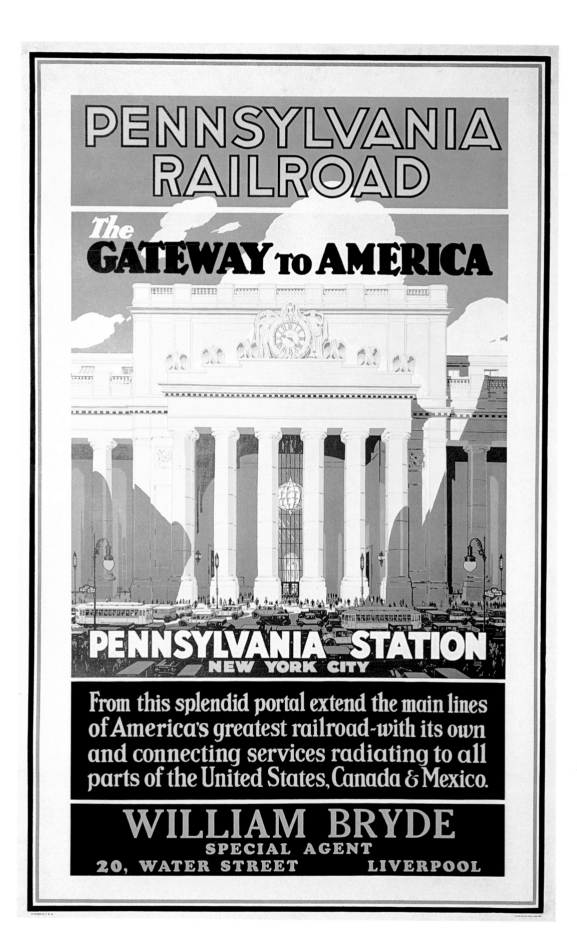

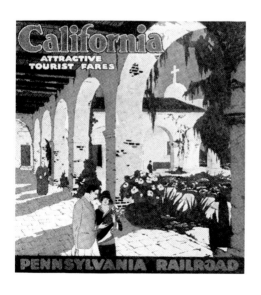

89

Fig. 115. N. C. Wyeth, July 1930. Swann Galleries.

Fig. 116. N. C. Wyeth, April 1932. *The Keystone,* Pennsylvania Railroad Technical & Historical Society.

NOTES

1. *The Poster,* Aug.1923, p. 22.

2. K. C. Ingram to P. Shoup, Sept. 13, 1928; K. C. Ingram to F. S. McGinnis, Nov. 5, 1928; SP Advertising Files, CSRM.

3. *Printers' Ink Monthly,* Dec. 1920, p. 27.

4. *Railway Age,* Sept. 3, 1927, p. 429.

5. *The Modern Poster Annual,* vol. 3, 1926–27.

6. *Western Advertising,* Jan. 1923, p. 108.

7. Leinard, "A Student Paints What He Sees," *Printed Salesmanship,* July 1931, p. 406.

8. SP's motto was derived from its unique structure: Its lines radiated north, east, and south from its San Francisco headquarters, whereas most railroads typically followed a single route.

9. Richmond, *The Technique of the Poster,* 1933, p. 70.

10. *Western Advertising,* Mar. 1921, p. 28; Dec. 1922, p. 32.

11. Daniels retired in 1907, died in July 1908; his protégé, P. V. D. Lockwood, succeeded him as advertising manager.

12. Bradshaw, p. 270.

13. *New York Central Lines Magazine,* July 1926, p. 39.

14. The New York City advertising firm Thomas F. Logan, Inc. merged with the San Francisco firm Lord & Thomas in 1926 to form Lord & Thomas and Logan.

15. *The Saturday Evening Post,* Oct. 9, 1926, p. 175.

16. Richmond, p. 83.

17. *Saturday Night,* Los Angeles, June 15, 1929, p. 2.

18. Southern Pacific Co. Advertising Files, K. C. Ingram to F. S. McGinnis, Jan. 17, 1927, CSRM.

19. *Advertising Age,* Oct. 26, 1936, p. 8.

20. Leinard, "A Master of Indian Portraiture," *Printed Salesmanship,* Nov. 1932, pp. 222–225, 256.

21. *The Poster,* July 1930, p. 13.

22. Couse Family Archives, W. H. Simpson to E. I. Couse: Apr. 15, 1931.

23. *The Poster,* Sept. 1916, p. 50.

24. Richmond, p. 157.

25. "Wm. Keith & his work . . . ," *Land of Sunshine,* May 1898, p. 255.

26. W. A. McKenzie to J. Gruber, Oct. 20, 1995; Walton, *The Burlington Northern Collection,* 1982, p. 37.

27. *Printers' Ink Monthly,* July 1925, pp. 27, 95.

28. S. Rea to W. W. Atterbury, Oct. 1, 1924, PRR presidents' files, Pa. State Archives.

29. PRR press release, May 22, 1930; I. Lee to W. W. Atterbury, quoted in *The Keystone,* spring 2001, p. 55. The other poster in the series was Nov. 1930, "Pittsburgh in the Beginning."

30. *The Pennsylvania News,* May 1, 1930, p. 1.

FIVE   The 1930s

[Modernism] is a young movement, but it is growing, and it expresses the present age just as art and architectural movements of the past have expressed the spirit of their ages.

—Joseph Binder

Depression-Era Innovation

In a 1934 interview, German expatriate artist Joseph Binder commented that the best American advertising art filled the covers and pages of magazines such as *Vanity Fair* and *Harper's Bazaar*. His interviewer pointed out that this was largely because mass circulation media continued to rule American advertising, whereas the poster dominated in Europe. Likewise, the American taste for what Binder termed "naturalistic" art continued unabated, giving only nodding recognition to the Modern movement that was transforming European design. Historian Weill agreed, characterizing American posters of the twenties and thirties as large, driven more by the national affinity for advertising slogans than eye-catching design. The grand prize winner at the First National Exhibit of Outdoor Advertising in 1930—Procter & Gamble's Oxydol soap poster of an African American woman carrying a basket of laundry as her mistress looked on approvingly, beneath the headline "Yes Ma'am—Jes' A Little!"—provided timely proof of their contention.[1]

Fortunately, travel poster artists were not nearly so set in their ways. *New York Times* writer John Markland contended in a 1936 article that travel posters "striking in color and design, are growing in favor as a means of depicting America's tourist attractions." The latest crop, he suggested, had finally overcome Americans' deep-seated attachment to realism and, instead, were characterized by "simplicity of design and subordination of detail to broad impressions." Like Treidler, he ascribed that conservatism to business's pragmatic outlook: "It is frequently said among American artists that American business men have been in the past too skeptical of anything smacking of the 'artistic' to contribute either money or encouragement to the development of poster art," he wrote. He closed with the prediction that "recent interest leads enthusiasts to expect that American artists and lithographers may soon have another opportunity to demonstrate on a wide scale what they can do to match Europe's poster output." Illustrations of the latest NP, SP, and NYC productions supported that optimistic outlook.[2]

A few railroads did follow the larger national trend and continued to experiment with billboards. Beginning in 1932, Southern Pacific pioneered auto-competitive billboards, targeting the private automobile with signs at points where highways came close to its tracks. SP's copy theme sold comfort: air conditioning and room to relax. Its message aggressively compared the two modes, suggesting, "Next Time, Try the Train." Evidently the line found them effective, as they ran well into the postwar years. In 1933, the Chesapeake & Ohio displayed its calendar phenomenon, Chessie the cat, paired with the slogan "Sleep like a Kitten," across the Midwest. One of the few railroad billboard campaigns to win professional recognition, it received Outdoor Advertising's third prize in 1934.

Leslie Ragan

Late in 1929, New York Central awarded a poster commission to Leslie Darrel Ragan, beginning a uniquely prolific and distinctive collaboration between railroad and artist. Although he worked for many transportation clients, Ragan's Central work stood apart. His series remained true to Central's strategy: depicting the natural landscape and cities along its route. The work itself was hallmarked by a striking use of color values and distillation of form that drew upon the heritage of the American illustrative tradition of Howard Pyle, Maxfield Parrish, and N. C. Wyeth. The collaboration spanned nearly twenty-five years and produced more than one hundred images. It came to identify the New York Central name in much the same way that Villa's Indian chief hallmarked the Santa Fe.

Ragan (1897–1972), who grew up in rural Iowa, was largely self-taught (fig. 117). He decided by age seven that he wanted to be an artist. "I was forever making drawings of buildings and bridges," he recalls in his unpublished autobiography.[3] Boyhood adventures exploring the Missouri River bluffs and among the mountains of Idaho also shaped his artistic vision. He served in the U.S. Army Air Force in France during World War I, although he never piloted a plane. Afterwards, he returned to Chicago, studied for a semester at the Art Institute of Chicago, and taught at the Academy of Fine Arts, Chicago's leading commercial art school, for four years, ca. 1921–24. There he was influenced by founder and famous cartoonist Carl N. Werntz, who had studied under Alphonse Mucha. By 1930 he had married and moved east to New York.

Ragan was a traditionalist. From the comfortable perspective of 1950, he reflected on art and the artists that shaped his career: "In those days, an artist was someone who painted pictures or sculpt in stone or

Fig. 117. (TOP) Leslie Ragan (*left*) receiving an award from Selective Service head General Hershey (*center*), for a wartime recruiting poster. The Society of Illustrators, New York City.

Fig. 118. (BOTTOM) Leslie Ragan's letterhead logo, ca. 1940. Helga Maurer Wagner collection.

bronze unlike today when anyone who bellows into a microphone or who squirts anything runnable onto any type of surface, may hang that tag on themselves." His work exemplified the American taste for realistic depiction while highlighting the natural environment for dramatic effect. He painted in opaque watercolor and was a virtuoso of light and shadow, a proficiency which enabled him to give his paintings a brilliance that played with natural effects: towering thunderheads, dramatic twilight shadows, shimmering waterborne reflections. Ragan's sense of composition and refined wash technique made his best images burst with reflected light. An avid sailor, he evidently found inspiration from the sea.

Ragan's Central poster style represented a maturation of his earlier work. During the late 1920s, as one of a half-dozen artists who designed posters for the Chicago South Shore & South Bend, an interurban line that traversed the scenic Lake Michigan coast, Ragan painted landscape views that showed the influence of his peers, as he experimented with color and form. In particular, he was influenced by Oscar Rabe Hanson (1901–1925), whose golden colors and pastoral images evoked heartland contentment.

Ragan's early NYC work was formal and traditional in conception; it focused on architecture, the outstanding example of Modernism in America. His first NYC poster, a cityscape of Chicago's Michigan Avenue dominated by a towering midday thunderhead, was produced late in 1929; its interplay of reflected light and building mass only hinted at what was to follow (fig. 119). His second, a sunset panorama marking the opening of the new Cleveland Union Terminal and tower, appeared in June 1930 (fig. 120). Ragan framed his subject with dark silhouettes of adjacent buildings, painting a dream-like sunset image bathed in fiery orange and lavender hues, alternating expanses of flat color with intense detail, a scheme that characterized his later work.

As the decade progressed, Ragan refined his style, simplifying both palette and form and developing the contrast of light and shadow that defined his best work. *West Point,* in 1934, made effective use of dramatic values, setting the academy's hulking mass against turquoise mountains and yellow sky (fig. 121). *Cincinnati,* a masterful depiction of urban rhythm and color, offset John A. Roebling's Ohio River suspension bridge with a modern skyline in 1935 (fig. 122). His range of subjects expanded to include the Hudson Valley, Adirondacks, and Niagara Falls landscapes, many of which NYC first produced as booklet covers (fig. 123). Ragan's work was so well received that when faced with Depression-era spending constraints, Central managers chose to retain his poster series while opting to discontinue their famous calendar. Throughout the decade he painted tens of poster images, finding the remarkable in mundane industrial cities—Eads Bridge at St. Louis, Boston's Old North Church, Cleveland's steel mills.

Ragan's cityscapes were particularly noteworthy for their dramatic perspective and powerful massing of Deco-styled skyscrapers.

Fig. 119. Leslie Ragan, 1929.

WEST POINT
UNITED STATES MILITARY ACADEMY
HIGHLANDS OF THE HUDSON

NEW YORK CENTRAL LINES

Fig. 120. (FACING PAGE) Leslie Ragan, 1930.
Swann Galleries.

Fig. 121. (ABOVE) Leslie Ragan, 1934.

Appropriately, his New York City images best communicated the sense of dynamic rhythm and energy emblematic of the skyscraper age. He shared this appreciation of the modern cityscape with John Held, Jr.; both drew multiple views of Manhattan icons—the RCA and Empire State Buildings—in the mid-thirties (figs. 124, 125, 126).

Ragan's reputation and following grew when the architectural journal *Pencil Points* published a dozen examples of his work in 1935, and selected his vista of downtown spires giving way to the New York harbor for its frontispiece (fig. 127). *Pencil Points*'s editor commented that Ragan's handling of values was "worthy of study by the architectural delineator."[4] *Advertising & Selling* seconded the opinion, offering Ragan's posters as "[e]vidence against the assertion that European travel posters are superior to American."[5] By 1936, Ragan's poster paintings of cityscapes had become so popular that the Central presented an exhibition on Grand Central's east balcony. However, the art and advertising community took only glancing notice of his work.

And, while *Pencil Points* hailed his powerful and rhythmic massing, it must be pointed out that Ragan traced some of his best-known panoramas. His *Upper Bay from Lower Manhattan* was borrowed from a photograph of the same title by Perry L. Sperr, taken from atop 60 Wall Street. And *Rockefeller Center,* ca. 1936, follows exactly artist John Wenrich's initial rendering of 1933 (aptly, Wenrich also rendered 60 Wall Street) (fig. 128).

Ragan kept largely to himself; he seldom discussed artistic influences or mentioned other artists. One notable exception was fellow poster designer Sascha Maurer, who kept a New York City studio within blocks of Ragan's and shared some of the same clients.

Snow Trains

One of the rails' most innovative and successful responses to the traffic loss of the early thirties were special snow and ski trains. First introduced by New England roads, they were heavily promoted with posters by local artists and quickly became a popular Depression-era phenomenon. The ski bug soon caught on in Manhattan where Saks Fifth Avenue and the New Haven co-sponsored their first New England "Snow Trains" in 1933. The service boomed: By 1935 the line estimated that Manhattan's skiing population had tripled to ten thousand. Shortly thereafter it commissioned Sascha Maurer, himself a skiing enthusiast, to advertise the trains. Maurer focused his designs on the sport's invigorating action appeal, creating a series of dynamic, eye-catching images that featured people with happy faces and in bright colors; in all a welcome escape from Depression-era drabness. His technique was determinedly modern: He made ample use of the air brush, and integrated typography into his designs; an early example spelled the word "Ski" as if it were ski tracks in the snow. Maurer's first Snow Train poster, "Let's go skiing!" appeared in the winter of 1936–37 and warranted rare notice

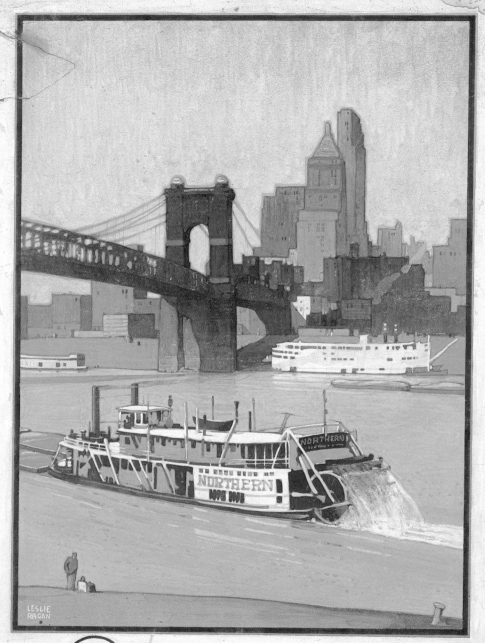

LESLIE RAGAN
NORTHERN
NORTHERN
CINCINNATI
ON THE OHIO
GATEWAY TO THE SOUTH
NEW YORK CENTRAL LINES

Fig. 122. (LEFT) Leslie Ragan, 1935, original artwork, opaque watercolor on board. Hugh T. Guillaume collection.

Fig. 123. (FACING PAGE) Leslie Ragan booklets, ca. 1934.

NEW YORK

LOWER MANHATTAN FROM THE UPPER BAY

NEW YORK CENTRAL LINES

Figs. 124 & 125. (LEFT) Leslie Ragan, New York and Chicago cityscapes, ca. 1934. New York Public Library.

Fig. 126. (ABOVE) Leslie Ragan, 1935.

Fig. 127. (FACING PAGE) Leslie Ragan, 1935. Swann Galleries.

NEW YORK THE UPPER BAY FROM LOWER MANHATTAN

NEW YORK CENTRAL SYSTEM

ROCKEFELLER CENTER
NEW YORK
NEW YORK CENTRAL LINES

in industry journals. The series continued through the prewar years (fig. 129).

Maurer was nearly unique among American artists in following the dictates of modern design. A German immigrant who arrived in New York City in 1925, Maurer (1898–1961) soon made himself one of the most influential voices in the campaign to improve poster design and broaden the medium's acceptance (fig. 130). Thoroughly schooled in the European tradition of graphic design, Maurer studied at the Munich Academy of Fine Arts under Hugo von Haberman and Angelo Jank and later journeyed to Brazil with the objective of mastering the lithographer's art. The 1925 offer of an apprentice position by artist Lucian Bernhard prompted his move to the United States. Maurer frequently spoke and wrote about poster design; he cited European masters Joseph Binder and A. M. Cassandre and Americans Otis Shepard and Jon Brubaker as important influences. In many ways, his opinions echoed those of fellow artist Adolph Treidler. Maurer decried the American penchant for "using monstrously enlarged paintings on posters" and questioned Americans' attachment to realistic illustration, which he disparaged as "rudimentary naturalism."[6]

While no record survives of how the New Haven found him, Maurer was by mid-decade a successful and recognized advocate of the medium. Likewise, the NH's publicity manager S. A. Boyer was promotionally adventurous. His was among the first lines to feature the slogan "Travel by Train" in its advertising. In addition to snow trains, NH ran cycle and pleasure-boat excursion trains, campaigned for incentives such as reduced fares, and bought hundreds of modern coaches designed by Walter Dorwin Teague, long before other eastern lines.[7]

The Streamliner Image

They are coming fast now. . . . It took the railroads so long to awake to the fact that the times were changing that one is a bit dazzled now by the brilliance with which they are translating that disarray into practice.

—*New York Herald Tribune,* June 30, 1936

The railroads were devastated by the Great Depression. Rail passenger-miles fell by half between 1929 and 1932, while automotive travel held its own. That alarming disparity spurred the industry into action, prompting an increasingly marketing-oriented outlook. By mid-1933, a few forward-thinking railroaders set an aggressive strategy of improvement, searching for more efficient designs that would increase speed and comfort while permitting reduced fares. As had their competitors in Detroit, they now turned to the new profession of industrial design.

Looking back, it is difficult to image the combination of risk and surprise that railroading's first two streamlining projects entailed. Union Pacific's M-10000, the first lightweight, air-flow train, made its

Fig. 128. (FACING PAGE) Leslie Ragan, ca. 1936. Posters Please, Inc.

Fig. 129. (ABOVE) Sascha Maurer, 1937.

Fig. 130. Sascha Maurer in his studio, ca. 1940. Helga Maurer Wagner collection.

debut in February 1934, at the Depression's nadir. Two months later, the Chicago, Burlington & Quincy's stainless-steel *Zephyr*, named for the god of the west wind, Zephyrus, followed. Both scored as immediate popular sensations. Indeed, they proved popular beyond the railroad men's wildest dreams, attracting millions trackside in hopes of gaining a glimpse of the future. Within a matter of days, their publicity tours brought out crowds of ten and twenty thousand daily; within months the Burlington estimated that two million had visited the three-car *Zephyr*. A year later, in May 1935, Union Pacific branded its expanding fleet with the "Streamliner" moniker, claiming a name that the public would apply to every new train that followed. As the decade progressed, streamlined trains proliferated, cutting travel times and offering new emphasis on comfort, luxury, and innovative design.

Americans, exhibiting their characteristic love of machines, embraced streamlining with an enthusiasm unmatched anywhere else in the world. Streamlined trains were among the most striking, visible, and accessible examples of Modernism, a style popularized in the mid-thirties by a growing corps of industrial designers. To the public the streamliner represented a welcome change from decades of uniformity: drab, dark green cars and dirty black locomotives. "The day coach received its present appearance a good many years ago," commented architect Paul Cret, who had designed the *Zephyr*'s interiors. Cret declared the streamliner to be the first distinctly new train since the "Pullman style of 1880." The designers' emphasis on aesthetics transformed the industry. Lucius Beebe, writing just two years after their introduction, concurred, declaring them a "dramatic symbol of a new era in railroading." The point was well taken. Even sixty-five years later, the first *Zephyr*'s styling retains its power; it "still looks like the future was supposed to look, exhibiting an efficiency that approaches grace."[8]

As plummeting passenger revenues decimated railroad advertising budgets, ad men, too, were forced to institute innovative, economical promotional strategies. Public equipment displays, high-speed press runs, live radio hook-ups, newsreel reports, and cooperative advertising campaigns were actively pursued. The poster medium—inexpensive and well suited to displaying "news"—also found increasing utility. Indeed, the streamliner was perfectly suited to the poster medium; its smooth airflow profile offered the prospect of a respite from America's stylistic preoccupation with realism. Poster artists responded enthusiastically, concentrating on the new trains' rakish styling and boldly colored paint schemes, producing stunning results.

Like the new trains themselves, the first streamliner posters were rushed into production. Given their transient purpose—to announce exhibition schedules—their production values were limited by austerity measures; only after the trains' initial success did elaborate posters appear. Union Pacific restricted advertising for the first streamliner's tours to black-and-white broadsides and newspaper and radio announcements. Plans for more aggressive publicity and poster advertis-

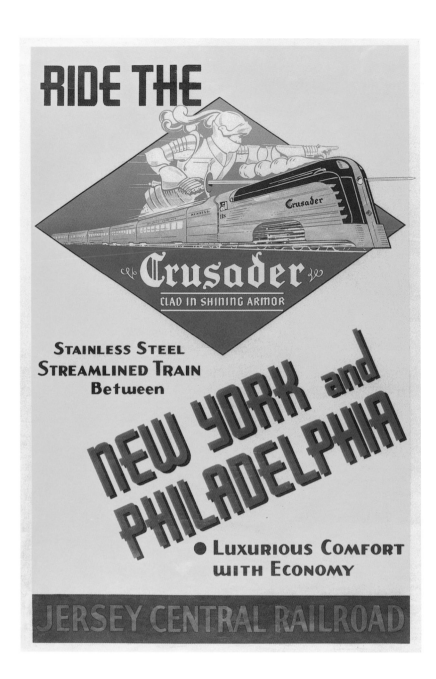

RIDE THE

Crusader
CLAD IN SHINING ARMOR

STAINLESS STEEL
STREAMLINED TRAIN
Between

NEW YORK and PHILADELPHIA

● LUXURIOUS COMFORT
WITH ECONOMY

JERSEY CENTRAL RAILROAD

Fig. 131. *The Crusader,* 1937, by an anonymous artist, vividly communicated the streamliners' appeal. The Huntington Library, San Marino, Calif., Leslie O. Merrill collection.

ing were canceled as the line found itself overwhelmed by crowds. The Burlington was initially inclined to follow suit: "I made it plain that we contemplate no display advertising, in as much as the UP experience indicates that more people show up without it than can be accommodated," wrote Burlington Passenger Traffic Manager (PTM) Albert Cotsworth, Jr., just weeks before the *Zephyr*'s debut.[9] Nevertheless, its more adventurous agency man, vice president Joseph H. Finn of Reincke-Ellis-Younggreen & Finn, produced an exhibition tour poster —a modern photographic collage depicting the airbrushed silver *Zephyr* as the latest in a parade of progress that began with the Conestoga wagon. The work also introduced the train's distinctive Art Deco logo of winged Zephyrus parting the clouds (fig. 132).

Perhaps the height of the streamliner mania was reached October 22–25, 1934, when millions watched the record-breaking fifty-six-hour transcontinental run of UP's second streamliner, the M-10001. *Time* hailed UP's newest as "no ordinary train"; terming it instead "the railroad's answer to aviation—a sleek streak of canary-yellow speed." Beebe wrote that it "suggest[ed] a sea monster that has been taken out of water and placed on wheels." If anything, such metaphors were more vivid than UP's poster design, most likely by the Willmarth studio of Omaha; of necessity, it emphasized form rather than color (fig. 133).[10]

Ironically, New York Central, traditionally at the forefront of passenger promotion, now found itself playing catch-up. Just weeks after the *Zephyr*'s introduction, Burlington publicity men proposed photographing their train alongside the fabled *20th Century.* Central's people, understandably embarrassed at being caught at the wrong end of the contrast between old and new, rather transparently suggested that "there is no opportunity." Belatedly, seven months later, in December 1934, NYC made its move by unveiling the *Commodore Vanderbilt,* the "World's first streamlined high powered steam locomotive." It, too, rated an exhibition poster: a modern photo collage that contrasted the gunmetal gray and aluminum *Commodore* with the line's first locomotive, the diminutive *DeWitt Clinton* (fig. 134).

As the railroaders rushed their streamliners into production, the advertising press pushed for more modern poster designs. To further suggest what might be done, in March 1935 *Advertising Arts* published two designs, which it termed "as modern as [the] things of today." In the first, under the banner "Go by Train," New York City designer Leo Rackow drew a city block of modern skyscrapers on the diagonal, bordered by a copy line of just two words: "New York." His second example set the words "air cooled" in clouds before a train that flew through space; while undeniably modern, it recalls William H. Bull's *Sunset Limited* design of nearly forty years before (fig. 135).[11]

By 1935 the industry began to display its creative mettle. Surprisingly, the staid Pullman Company, which had last advertised in 1917, was among the first to respond to the encroaching competition. According to *Fortune* magazine, Pullman's aversion to innovation had become

Fig. 132. C. N. Johnson, 1934.

Fig. 133. Union Pacific, 1934, anonymous.

WORLD'S FIRST STREAMLINED HIGH POWERED STEAM LOCOMOTIVE

NEW YORK CENTRAL LINES

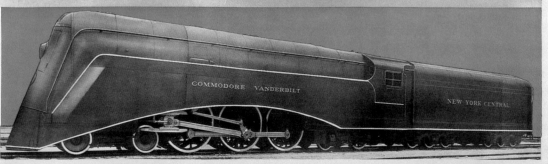

PUBLIC EXHIBITION · LA SALLE STREET STATION, CHICAGO

JANUARY 12, 8 am to 10 pm
JANUARY 13, 8 am to 2 pm

Fig. 134. (LEFT) New York Central, 1934, anonymous. Hugh T. Guillaume collection.

Fig. 135. (FACING PAGE TOP) Leo Rackow, 1935. New York Public Library.

Fig. 136. (FACING PAGE BOTTOM) William Welsh, 1935, 21" x 27".

road names with the new slogan. Meanwhile, back east, the Pennsylvania produced a notable Deco-styled poster selling Washington, D.C. by calendar artist Grif Teller, who prominently featured the capital's two latest improvements—the new Supreme Court building and PRR's latest streamlined electric locomotive (fig. 139).

The Southern Pacific Studio

Southern Pacific was a partner with Union Pacific in the original Overland Route of 1869, and the two lines cooperated as a matter of course in pioneering transcontinental streamliners. Beginning in 1936, SP advertising manager F. Q. Tredway produced a new thematic image —bold speed-styled profiles now identified SP posters and newspaper and magazine ads.

Southern Pacific's designs were the collaborative effort of a team of artists who created dynamic images that emphasized the trains' dramatic

the object of national ridicule, "like Philadelphia, the stock in trade of comedians." Pullman may have been reluctant to embark upon the wholesale replacement of its venerable dark green fleet, but that outlook did not preclude advertising.

Between 1935 and 1938, Pullman vice-president James Kelly, who had long been fascinated by European travel posters, commissioned nearly a dozen poster designs by Chicago artist William P. Welsh (1889–?). His intent was to promote the company's unmatched safety record and the comfort of its increasingly air-conditioned fleet. Welsh had studied at the Academie Julien in Paris and had made a name for himself painting the mural decorations in the Chicago Room of that city's famed Palmer House and by winning the competition to design the 1933 Chicago World's Fair poster. As Pullman operated only a handful of streamlined cars, Welsh chose instead to feature its patrons: stylish women whom he posed in serene outdoor settings. He bathed his subjects in brilliant color and rendered their surroundings in Art Deco–styled patterns: rippling lakes, swirling waterfalls, rolling hills dotted with trees. Produced as posters, car cards, and window hangers, Welsh's campaign won widespread public recognition and several design awards (figs. 136, 137, 138).

Out West, a coalition of nearly thirty railroads pooled their resources against the auto and introduced the "Travel by Train" campaign. Their cooperative effort produced nearly a dozen posters portraying a range of national destinations. Most notable were *New York's Fifth Avenue* by Fred Mizen and western landscapes by Denver artist H. M. Veenstra and Oscar Bryn. Again dictates of austerity made themselves felt as other lines recast time-tested images by replacing individual rail-

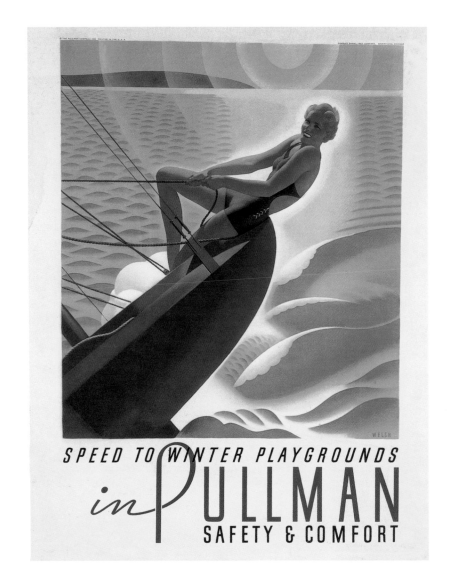

TRAVEL AT REDUCED RATES TO YOUR FAVORITE
SUMMER RESORT
IN *Pullman* SAFETY & COMFORT

TRAVEL AT REDUCED RATES TO YOUR FAVORITE
SUMMER RESORT
IN *Pullman* SAFETY & COMFORT

automotive-inspired profiles and brilliant color schemes. Their family resemblance stemmed from the fact that one man, German-born draftsman Morris Rehag, rendered their streamlined forms. Color was later added by Fred Ludekens, senior art director at SP's ad agency, Lord & Thomas and Logan, and associates Haines Hall (1903–1977) and Paul Carey. Hall had started out in a newspaper art department, as had many of his contemporaries, and later joined the San Francisco commercial art firm of Patterson & Sullivan. His work first appeared in *Western Advertising* in 1933. Carey, who also hailed from Patterson & Sullivan, later became a business partner with Maurice Logan and the two often painted together on weekends; Ludekens's great inspiration and mentor had been Louis Treviso.

SP's first streamliner poster, designed in 1936, emphasized the distinctive "armor yellow" color and automotive profile of the new *City of San Francisco* (fig. 140). The artists communicated modernity and speed by rendering the train in a seamless watercolor wash, removing all trace of rivets and vestibules. The following year they designed an equally striking rendition of the new *Daylight* streamliner (fig. 141). The train's outstanding characteristic was its brilliant red, orange, and black paint scheme, drawn from the California landscape; *Fortune* magazine termed it "circusy." With its locomotive raked forward to denote speed, a wisp of airbrushed white exhaust floated against a deep blue sky. Stylized clouds and an undulating zigzag trace of mountains completed the design. *Western Advertising* noted "a trace of the dynamic, dramatic technique of the European travel poster" in the work.[11]

The SP studio produced streamliner images through the early war years, but as the new trains became increasingly common their themes reverted to the traditional appeals of scenery and distinctive creature comforts: new Polaroid windows, extra-long berths. Still, Haines Hall created a dramatic modern rendition of a streamliner in *Crossing Great Salt Lake* and Canadian artist Ray Bethers designed scenes of "Old Mexico" that gained notice of the New York Art Directors Club (fig. 142). When SP's postwar trains arrived, they were set in traditional western settings by Fred Ludekens.

Sascha Maurer: The Appeal of the Machine

Sascha Maurer's work most closely approximated the European style; his designs emphasized the tangible consumer appeal of the new technology—speed and power. In this he drew upon the work of A. M. Cassandre, who in the late 1920s had moved the travel poster away from portraying destinations and instead visualized the appeal of the machine: massive driving wheels, swirling steam, receding rails.

When in spring 1937 the New Haven decided to commemorate its fiftieth birthday with a poster, it again turned to Maurer. As the new steam locomotives which were to be the work's inspiration were still under construction, Maurer visited the Baldwin Locomotive Works in

Fig. 137. (FACING PAGE TOP) William Welsh, 1935, 21" x 27".

Fig. 138. (FACING PAGE BOTTOM) William Welsh, 1935, 21" x 27". Swann Galleries.

Fig. 139. (ABOVE) Grif Teller, 1935.

Fig. 140. (ABOVE LEFT) Southern Pacific Studio, 1936, 16" x 23". California State Railroad Museum.

Fig. 141. (FACING PAGE) Southern Pacific Studio, 1937. The Huntington Library, San Marino, Calif., Leslie O. Merrill collection.

Fig. 142. (ABOVE RIGHT) Haines Hall, 1940, 16" x 23".

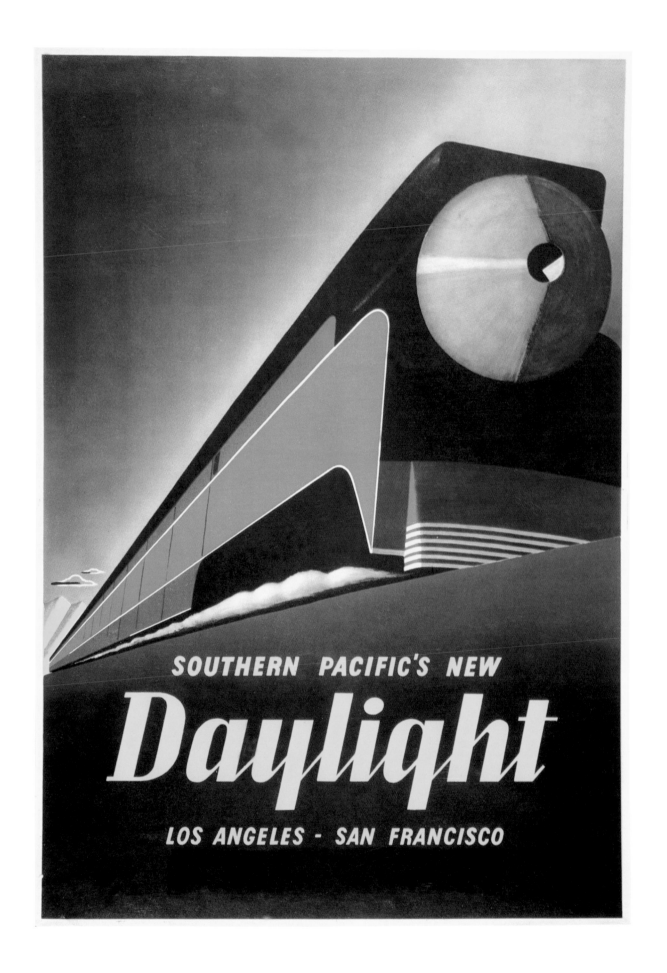

Philadelphia to ride and sketch the first engine. During the two-hour train ride back to his Manhattan studio he sketched ideas; four hours later, he had his image.

Fortunately, the New Haven saved Maurer's developmental sketches in order to demonstrate his creative process, the link between initial conception and finished work (fig. 143). They indicate that he was quite aware of other streamliner poster designs. Like SP's Rehag, Maurer distilled the streamliner form down to its barest essentials, eliminating handrails, rivets, and coupler. Maurer was most impressed with the locomotive's scale and power; thus the headline "Greater Power." When finished, his hulking black locomotive appeared to have steamed out of a cloud, the embodiment of machine-age speed and energy (fig. 144).

Maurer's forceful image—his focus on the sheer power and thrill of technology—won more praise from advertising professionals than any other railroad design of its era. The Brooklyn Museum included it in a contemporary exhibition of "pictures and designs that work." It was shown in the annual New York Art Directors Club Exhibition and published in the club's 1938 Annual. NH bragged that the work "was recognized in advertising circles as having all the elements of a great poster: simplicity, strength, and legibility from a distance."

Other Maurer maquettes provide further perspective into the process of balancing a commercial message with artistic impulse. In designing *Summer in New England*, probably in 1938, he first proposed a conventional layout, placing a train before a scenic background (fig. 145); but the produced poster drew on the success of *Greater Power*, filling the locomotive's image with seacoast scenery. Maurer's finished design communicated the ideas of modernity and vacation fun in one remarkable image. It is one of the few American poster designs to effectively integrate appeal of technology and destination (fig. 146).

Maurer tried much the same with his other railroad client, the PRR, in 1939. PRR had hired him to illustrate its unique direct rail link to the New York World's Fair. Maurer proposed to feature the PRR's distinctive new electric locomotive, which had recently been streamlined by Raymond Loewy, in much the same way, but the PRR's conservative managers would have nothing to do with it (fig. 147). Instead, they chose to produce a more conventional and less effective layout that relied on a stylized map rather than a machine image (fig. 148).

If Maurer was less than satisfied with *Direct Route*, subsequent PRR commissions proved more rewarding. He featured both *Atlantic City* (ca. 1940), a signature happy female face, the famed boardwalk reflected in her sunglasses, and 1941's *The Jeffersonian*, with red, white, and blue patriotism, on his promotional cards (figs. 149, 150). He was likewise proud of the wartime poster *Washington*, which framed the capitol dome with a single Doric column, his metaphor for the solidity of Democracy.

A 1940 PRR poster commissioned to promote *The South Wind*, a Florida streamliner, also follows Maurer's style but is missing a

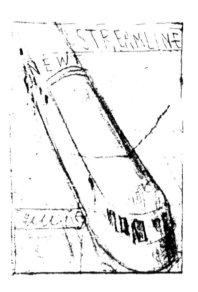

Fig. 143. (FACING PAGE AND ABOVE) Sascha Maurer's developmental sketches for *Greater Power*. Helga Maurer Wagner collection.

Fig. 144. (RIGHT) Sascha Maurer, 1938.

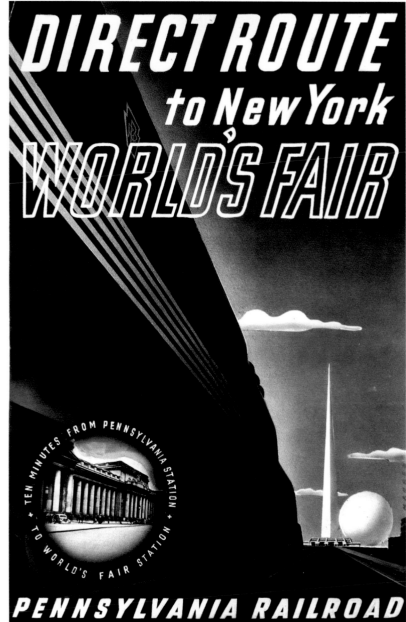

Fig. 145. (ABOVE LEFT) Sascha Maurer maquette for *Summer in New England*, ca. 1938.

Fig. 146. (FACING PAGE) Sascha Maurer, 1938.

Fig. 147. (ABOVE RIGHT) Sascha Maurer maquette for *Direct Route*, 1939.

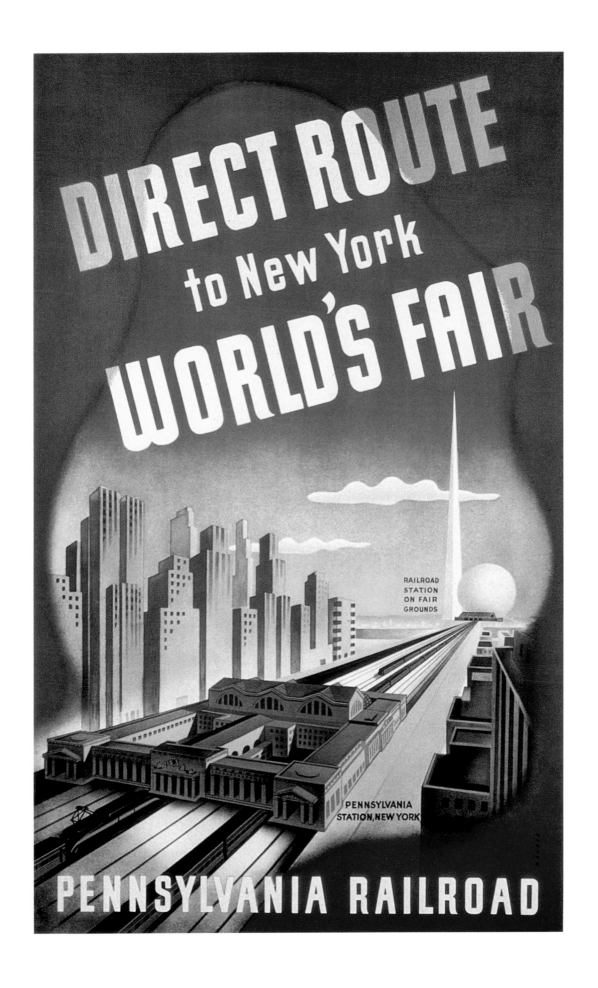

Fig. 148. (FACING PAGE) Sascha Maurer, 1939. The Mitchell Wolfson Jr. Collection, The Wolfsonian-Florida International University.

Fig. 149. (BELOW) Sascha Maurer, ca. 1940. Swann Galleries.

Fig. 150. (RIGHT) Sascha Maurer, 1941.

Fig. 151. Pennsylvania Railroad, 1940, anonymous. *The Keystone*, Pennsylvania Railroad Technical & Historical Society.

Fig. 152. Leslie Ragan, 1938.

Fig. 153. Leslie Ragan, 1939. Swann Galleries.

Fig. 154. Leslie Ragan, 1941.

signature (fig. 151). Its artist made characteristic use of the air brush, bold block lettering, and an arrow-like train to effectively communicate the new train's route and speed. It attests that PRR managers had come to believe (and act upon) the ad press's assertion that "Streamline is the fashion today. . . . " Unfortunately the line would never again produce such modern posters.

Artist Maurer, meanwhile, met with increasing success. He designed corporate trademarks and lectured and designed at New York's Society of Illustrators. His list of clients grew to include Quaker State and Standard Oil, Lucky Strike, and the states of Connecticut and Vermont. In 1941 the editors of *Encyclopedia Britannica* contacted him to propose the use of his Lake Placid ski poster as the illustration for the article "poster."

Ragan's Streamliners

Leslie Ragan set the new trains in surreal landscapes, bathing their reflective surfaces in shimmering natural light, creating dream-like poster icons. In June 1938 the new *20th Century Limited,* designed from locomotive to matchbook cover by New York City industrial designer Henry Dreyfuss, made its debut. To mark the occasion, Ragan created a poster that became the archetype of American streamliner designs (fig. 152). His rendering left locomotive driving wheels and gadgetry in shadow, instead focusing on the *Century*'s distinctive satin-finished crescent-shaped prow as it caught the morning sunlight while steaming alongside the Hudson River, New York City–bound. ("One of the most distinctive pieces of mechanism ever seen on any track," bragged Central publicists.) Dreyfuss had designed a dignified two-tone gray paint scheme for NYC's new flagship, and Ragan made its reflection dance in the river's shimmering water; Central was, after all, "the water level route."

That same year, a consortium of North American railroads and the Pullman Company commissioned Ragan to design posters promoting both the New York World's Fair and San Francisco's Golden Gate International Exposition. *See America* depicted a panoramic collage of iconic American images that ranged from Indian chief to California mission and heartland bounty (fig. 153). The silhouette of a streamlined steam locomotive designed for the Pennsylvania by Raymond Loewy dominated *Railroads on Parade,* commissioned by the eastern railroads.

When Central streamlined the *Empire State Express,* Ragan set the train in the Hudson River Highlands on an autumn afternoon (fig. 154). Locomotive driving wheels and apparatus are lost in a blur while elegantly fluted stainless-steel passenger cars reflect the day's waning light. In the background, mountains cast in brilliant hues of red and orange dominate. Ironically, the new streamliner made its debut on December 7, 1941, the day of Japan's attack at Pearl Harbor. Railroading and advertising were about to change forever.

NOTES

1. *Printed Salesmanship,* Nov. 1934, pp. 122–125; Nov. 1930, p. 213.
2. *The New York Times,* Feb. 9, 1936, IX, p. 9.
3. The authors wish to thank Marilyn Hinners for sharing Ragan's family documents.
4. *Pencil Points,* June 1935, inside front cover.
5. *Advertising & Selling,* Feb. 14, 1935, p. 21.
6. *The Advertiser,* Jan. 1932, p. 20.
7. *Printers' Ink Monthly,* June 1937, p. 128.
8. Robert Campbell in *The New York Times Book Review,* Jan. 14, 2001.
9. A. Cotsworth, Jr., to H. F. McLaury, Mar. 2, 1934, CB&Q collection, Newberry Library.
10. *Time,* Nov. 5, 1934; *Town & Country,* June 1936, pp. 50–55.
11. *Advertising Arts,* Mar. 1935, p. 28.
12. *Western Advertising,* Oct. 1937, p. 27.

Postscript

I see gorgeous drawings of the train of tomorrow, which is to have frequency modulation I don't want and a pretty hostess to amuse the children I don't travel with, but the Pullman Palace Car goes on soiling my shirt, tiring me out with badly designed cushions, and bouncing so much I can't work on my proofs.

—Bernard DeVoto[1]

The streamliner era also brought disappointment. The Santa Fe's pioneering ad man William H. Simpson passed away in 1933, and was shortly followed by his protégé, Carl Birchfield, in 1936. Their successor, Roger Birdseye, continued the line's romantic southwestern advertising theme, and provided much of the inspiration for the famous *Super Chief* of 1937, one of the most remarkable trains of all time. Its red-and-silver diesel locomotives were painted in a design that was intended to resemble an Indian chief's warbonnet, while its interiors replicated ancient Navajo and Hopi designs. However, the Depression had shorn Santa Fe's advertising of its vivid color. The line continued to produce posters throughout the thirties, yet the images were now dull sepia-colored photos.

In the aftermath of Pearl Harbor, the streamliner images vanished as American railroad advertising assumed a somber, patriotic attitude. Wartime also inspired memorable images: A Leslie Ragan poster set a massive New York Central *Mohawk* locomotive against a night sky and the Statue of Liberty's torch (fig. 155). Edwin Georgi's *The Kid in Upper 4,* a New Haven print ad and poster that recounted a young recruit's fears and dreams on his way to war, produced a wave of popular emotion (fig. 156). George Lerner and Lyman Powers's award-winning SP billboard design likened a speeding locomotive to a shining bayonet (fig. 157). Even so, wartime delays and crowding soured the nation's recollection of the railroads' heroic World War II performance.

Looking to the postwar marketplace, the rails addressed their shortcomings in advertising that promised new amenities and innovations, most memorably the glass-topped vista dome car. But few posters were produced, and those that were became lost in an avalanche of four-color

magazine pages; those posters that were created focused largely on consumer comforts. One bright exception was NYC, which in 1947 commissioned Leslie Ragan to design a poster view of the Hudson River Highlands at twilight (fig. 158). Unfortunately, the work was nearly the last of a long collaboration; now at the top of his career Ragan painted on the Mediterranean island of Majorca, working from photos sent to him by clients. His work for a new railroad client, the Budd Company, a manufacturer of patented stainless-steel passenger cars, was now nationally known and as distinctive as his bold blue "LR" letterhead. Indeed, in 1946, art editor Ernest W. Watson counted Ragan among the nation's forty top illustrators and named him the leading transportation artist, although by then scant competition remained.

Santa Fe also defied the trend: Its final series of posters, produced in 1949–50, featured colorful images of California beaches, Texas cattle brands, "Hopiland," and, of course, the Grand Canyon rendered in Oscar Bryn's vivid hues (figs. 159, 160). "Bryn had a fine appreciation of the Southwest and his style of work—bold colors and unusual compositions—set it off from other artists," recalled Fred Tipple, Santa Fe's last advertising manager to promote passenger trains. "He continued to paint posters for the Santa Fe from his home in Oakland, California,—I believe he passed away in the 1960's."[2] (Bryn died in 1967.)

Other lines, notably NH, UP, and PRR, continued to produce posters through the mid-1950s. New Haven continued New England resort themes, now designed by New England artist Ben Nason; Union Pacific sold *Streamliners,* skiing at Sun Valley, and the national parks, many designed by Omaha's Willmarth studio; the Pennsylvania promoted historic Middle Atlantic cities and its flyer, the *Broadway Limited* (figs. 161, 162). Surprisingly, the fifties' best poster designs came from a most unexpected source. General Motors's locomotive-manufacturing subsidiary produced a poster campaign targeted at the industry's purchasing agents, designed by Connecticut artist Bern Hill (1911–1977).

Like Ragan, Hill termed himself a traditionalist; he greatly admired Andrew Wyeth, but felt "slightly suspicious about other modern trends." He rendered GM locomotives in boldly colored landscape settings from striking perspectives. Unfortunately, the work was not widely distributed and received little popular notice (fig. 163).

In the spring of 1950, Sascha Maurer contacted Leslie Ragan in hopes of finding potential railroad clients. "I mentioned you to Jim Bishop [of Lewis & Gillman, for whom Ragan painted Budd Co.

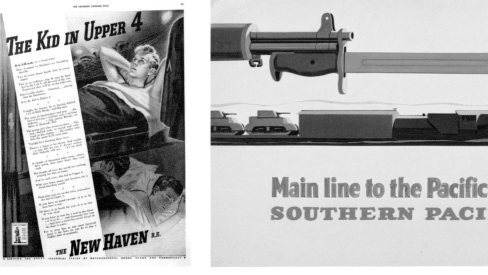

Fig. 155. (FACING PAGE TOP) Leslie Ragan, 1943.

Fig. 156. (FACING PAGE BOTTOM LEFT) Edwin Georgi, 1942, reproduced as magazine ad.

Fig. 157. (FACING PAGE BOTTOM RIGHT) Billboard, George Lerner and Lyman Powers, 1945. California State Railroad Museum.

Fig. 158. (RIGHT) Leslie Ragan, 1947.

HIGHLANDS OF THE HUDSON

NEW YORK CENTRAL SYSTEM

Fig. 159. Don Perceval, 1949,
18" x 24".

Fig. 160. Oscar Bryn, 1949, 18" x 24".

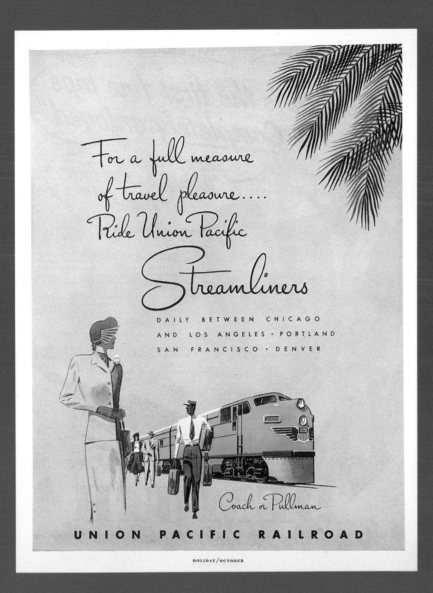

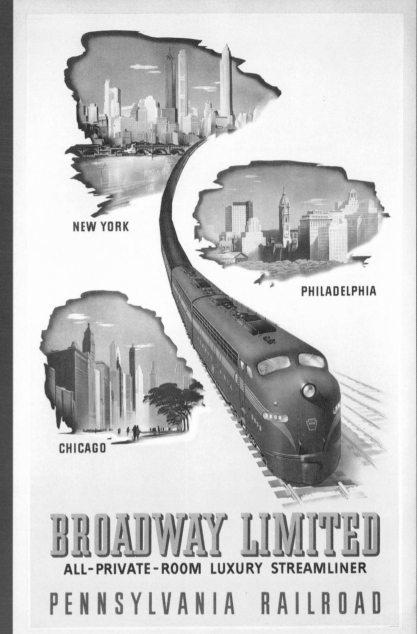

Fig. 161. (ABOVE LEFT) William Willmarth, 1949.

Fig. 162. (ABOVE RIGHT) Pennsylvania Railroad, 1953, anonymous.

Fig. 163. (FACING PAGE) Bern Hill, ca. 1950. California State Railroad Museum.

advertisements] the other day," Ragan replied. "He knows your work, of course, and seemed quite interested that you are going to call on him."[3] However, no commission followed; the railroad advertising field had dried up. Perhaps it was just as well. By 1952 the railroad as a mode of travel was in deep eclipse; that year, for the first time, more people traveled by airplane than by Pullman car. "The railroad always has so much to offer in the way of pictorially picturesque material," remarked illustrator and art director W. Livingston Larned in 1928, in introducing the New York Central's art poster campaign, "It is the stuff of which popular appeal is made."[4] But that taste had changed; now Americans looked forward to a spin in a new Ford and a cruise on a TWA *Starliner*.

NOTES

1. DeVoto, "The Easy Chair," *Harper's*, Apr. 1947, p. 335.
2. Phone interview, Jan. 1997.
3. Leslie Ragan to Sascha Maurer, Apr. 23, 1950, Maurer Family Archives.
4. *Printers' Ink Monthly*, July 1928, p. 51.

Fig. 164. Baltimore & Ohio, 1949, anonymous.

BIBLIOGRAPHY

Overwhelmingly, published works about travel posters focus on the medium's development in Europe. Comment on and analysis of American poster development is found in American advertising periodicals, of which there were dozens at the turn of the century.

Books

Armitage, Merle. 1986. Reprint. *Homage to the Santa Fe.* Hawthorne, Calif.: Omni Publications. Original edition, Yucca Valley, Calif.: Manzanita Press, 1973.

Battersby, Martin. 1988. Revised edition. *The Decorative Twenties.* London: Herbert Press. Original edition, London: Studio Vista, 1969.

————. 1988. Revised edition. *The Decorative Thirties.* London: Herbert Press. Original edition, London: Studio Vista, 1971.

Beebe, Lucius Morris. 1962. *20th Century: The Greatest Train in the World.* Berkeley: Howell-North.

————. 1963. *The Central Pacific & the Southern Pacific Railroads.* Berkeley: Howell-North.

————. 1963. *The Overland Limited.* Berkeley: Howell-North.

Beebe, Lucius, and Charles Clegg. [1965] 1966. *The Trains We Rode,* vols. I and II. Berkeley: Howell-North.

Boas, Nancy. 1988. *The Society of Six: California Colorists.* San Francisco: Bedford Arts Publishers.

Borges, Jorge Luis. 1998. *Collected Fictions.* New York: Penguin Putnam.

Bradshaw, Percy V. 1925. *Art in Advertising: A Study of British and American Pictorial Publicity.* London: The Press Art School.

Calkins, Earnest Elmo. 1946. *"And hearing not—": Annals of an Adman.* New York: Charles Scribner's Sons.

Choko, Marc H., and David L. Jones. 1995. *Canadian Pacific Posters: 1883–1963.* Ottawa: Meridian Press.

Cohen, Ronald D., and Stephen G. McShane. 1998. *Moonlight in Duneland: The Illustrated Story of the Chicago South Shore and South Bend Railroad.* Bloomington: Indiana University Press.

Cole, Beverly, and Richard Durack. 1992. *Railway Posters, 1923–1947: From the Collection of the National Railway Museum, York, England.* New York: Rizzoli.

Connelly, Marc, and Carl J. Weinhardt. 1972. *The Most of John Held, Jr.* Brattleboro, Vt.: The Stephen Greene Press.

Cupper, Dan. 1992. *Crossroads of Commerce: The Pennsylvania Railroad Calendar Art of Grif Teller.* Richmond, Vt.: Great Eastern Publishing.

D'Emilio, Sandra, and Suzan Campbell. 1991. *Visions & Visionaries: The Art & Artists of the Santa Fe Railway.* Salt Lake City: Peregrine Smith.

Dixon, Thomas W. 1988. *Chessie: The Railroad Kitten.* Lynchburg, Va.: TLC Publishing.

Dubin, Arthur D. 1964. *Some Classic Trains.* Milwaukee: Kalmbach.

———. 1974. *More Classic Trains.* Milwaukee: Kalmbach.

Ellis, Cuthbert Hamilton. 1959. *British Railway History: An Outline from the Accession of William IV to the Nationalization of Railways, 1877–1947.* London: Allen and Unwin.

Falk, Peter H. 1985. *Who Was Who in American Art.* Madison, Conn.: Sound View Press.

Gallo, Max. 1974. *The Poster in History.* New York: American Heritage Publishing Co.; distributed by McGraw-Hill.

Goodrum, Charles A., and Helen Dalrymple. 1990. *Advertising in America: The First 200 Years.* New York: Harry N. Abrams.

Hagerty, Donald J. 1993. *Desert Dreams: The Art and Life of Maynard Dixon.* Salt Lake City: Gibbs-Smith Publisher.

Halsey, Ashley, Jr. 1951. *Illustrating for* The Saturday Evening Post. Boston: Arlington House.

Heyman, Therese Thau. 1998. *Posters American Style.* New York: National Museum of American Art, Smithsonian Institution, in association with H.N. Abrams.

Hillier, Bevis. 1976. *Travel Posters.* New York: E.P. Dutton.

Johnson, J. Stewart. 2000. *American Modern, 1925–1940: Design for a New Age.* New York: Harry N. Abrams.

Johnson, Lynn, and Michael O'Leary. 1999. *All Aboard! Images from the Golden Age of Rail Travel.* San Francisco: Chronicle Books.

Jones, William C., Harry H. Buckwalter, and Elizabeth B. Jones. 1989. *Buckwalter: The Colorado Scenes of a Pioneer Photojournalist, 1890–1920.* Boulder, Colo.: Pruett Publishing.

Kurutz, KD, and Gary F. Kurutz. 2000. *California Calls You: The Art of Promoting the Golden State, 1870 to 1940.* Sausalito: Windgate Press.

Leavitt, Virginia Couse. 1991. *Eanger Irving Couse: Image Maker for America.* Albuquerque: The Albuquerque Museum.

Levenson, Michael, ed. 1999. *The Cambridge Companion to Modernism.* New York: Cambridge University Press.

Lomazzi, Brad S. 1995. *Railroad Timetables, Travel Brochures & Posters.* Spencertown, N.Y.: Golden Hill Press.

Margolin, Victor. 1975. *American Poster Renaissance: The Great Age of American Poster Design, 1890–1900.* New York: Watson-Guptill.

Margolin, Victor, Ira Brichta, and Vivian Brichta. 1979. *The Promise and the Product: 200 Years of American Advertising Posters.* New York: Macmillan.

Marshall, James. 1945. *Santa Fe: The Railroad That Built an Empire.* New York: Random House.

Martin, Albro. 1971. *Enterprise Denied: Origins of the Decline of American Railroads, 1897–1917.* New York: Columbia University Press.

Mühl, Albert, and Jürgen Klein. 1998. *125 Years International Sleeping Car Company: Trains de Luxe—History and Posters.* Bonn: VG-Bild-Kunst.

Nolan, Edward W. 1983. *Northern Pacific Views: The Railroad Photography of F. Jay Haynes, 1876–1905.* Helena: Montana Historical Society Press.

Norris, James D. 1990. *Advertising and the Transformation of American Society, 1865–1920.* New York: Greenwood Press.

Pangborn, J. G. 1883. *Picturesque Baltimore & Ohio.* Chicago: Knight & Leonard.

Pomeroy, Earl S. 1957. *In Search of the Golden West: The Tourist in Western America.* New York: Knopf.

Pratt, Edwin A. 1903. *American Railways.* London, New York: Macmillan and Co.

Presbrey, Frank. [1929] 1966. *The History and Development of Advertising.* Garden City, N.Y.: Doubleday, Doran and Co.

Price, Charles Matlack. [1913] 1929. *Posters: A Critical Study.* New York: G.W. Bricka.

Reed, Walt, and Roger Reed. 1984. *The Illustrator in America, 1880–1980.* New York: Published for the Society of Illustrators by Madison Square Press.

Repp, Stan. 1980. *The Super Chief . . . Train of the Stars.* San Marino, Calif.: Golden West Books.

Richmond, Leonard, ed. 1933. *The Technique of the Poster.* London: Sir Isaac Pitman & Sons.

Rowe, Vivian. 1958. *French Railways of To-day.* London: George G. Harrap and Co.

Runte, Alfred. 1990. *Trains of Discovery: Western Railroads and the National Parks.* Niwot, Colo.: Robert Rinehart Publishers.

Schwantes, Carlos A. 1993. *Railroad Signatures across the Pacific Northwest.* Seattle: University of Washington Press.

Staufer, Alvin F., and Edward L. May. 1974. *Thoroughbreds: New York Central's 4-6-4 Hudson.* Medina, Ohio: Staufer.

Steele, H. Thomas. 1989. *Lick 'Em, Stick 'Em: The Lost Art of Poster Stamps.* New York: Abbeville Press.

Stern, Jean, and Ruth Westphal. 1980. *The Paintings of Sam Hyde Harris (1889–1977).* Beverly Hills, Calif.: Petersen Galleries.

Stilgoe, John R. 1983. *Metropolitan Corridor: Railroads and the American Scene.* New Haven: Yale University Press.

Strauss, Steve. 1984. *Moving Images: The Transportation Poster in America.* New York: Fullcourt Press.

Thomas, W. Donald. 1992. *Airline Artistry: Vintage Posters & Publicity.* Dunedin, Fla.: W.D. Thomas.

Walton, Ann Thorson. 1982. *The Burlington Northern Collection.* St. Paul, Minn.: Burlington Northern.

Warner, Charles Dudley. 1891. *Our Italy.* New York: Harper & Brothers.

Watson, Ernest W. 1946. *Forty Illustrators and How They Work.* New York: Watson-Guptill.

Weigle, Marta, and Barbara A. Babcock, eds. 1996. *The Great Southwest of the Fred Harvey Company and the Santa Fe Railway.* Phoenix, Ariz.: The Heard Museum.

Weill, Alain. 1985. *The Poster: A Worldwide Survey and History.* Boston: G.K. Hall.

———. 1994. *L'Invitation au voyage: l'affiche de tourisme dans le monde.* Paris: Editions Somogy.

Wheeler, Olin Dunbar. 1893–1906. *Wonderland.* St. Paul, Minn.: Northern Pacific Railway.

Articles

DeVoto, Bernard. 1947. "The Easy Chair." *Harper's* (April): 335.

Duverney, Paul. 1899. "Railway Posters." *The Poster* [London] (August): 277–285.

"Excellent Railway Advertising." *The Advertising World* (April 1917).

"How the SP Advertises." *The Graphic Arts* (December 1911): 20.

Kimber, Sidney A. 1925. "Foreign Travel Posters." *Printed Salesmanship* XLVI, no. 2: 134–136.

Larned, W. Livingston. 1928. "New York Central Lines Pioneer in Railroad Poster Advertising." *Printers' Ink Monthly* (July): 51, 120–125.

Leinard, Augusta. 1931. "A Student Paints What He Sees—An Artist Paints What He Knows!" *Printed Salesmanship* (July): 406–410, 440–441.

———. 1932. "A Master of Indian Portraiture." *Printed Salesmanship* (November): 222–225, 256.

"On Railway Advertising." *Printers' Ink* (April 1899): 3–4.

Pollard, Percival. 1899. "American Poster Lore." *The Poster* (March): 123.

"Poster Exhibit Stimulates Travel." *Railway Age* 87, no. 10, 1929.

Price, C. Matlack. 1916. "The Poster as an Artistic Ally in the Advertising of American Cities." *Current Opinion* (April): 277–279.

"Publisher's Page." *Sunset* (February 1900): 167.

"Railway Advertising." *Printers' Ink* (February 1892): 147, 148.

"See Europe First." *Judge* (January 1913).

"Wm. Keith & his work . . ." *Land of Sunshine* (May 1898): 255.

Booklets and Serials

Phelps, Henry P. 1902. *Golden State Limited* inaugural booklet (November). Rock Island System.

Young & McCallister, Inc. 1916. *The Needle.* Los Angeles. Monthly serial.

Periodicals

The Advertiser

Advertising Age, Chicago

Advertising & Selling, New York

Advertising Arts, Chicago

Advertising Experience, Chicago

The Advertising World, London

Art in Advertising, New York

The Artist & Advertiser, Chicago

The Artist and Adviser, New York

The Bill Poster, New York

The Billposter and Distributor, New York and Chicago

Brush and Pencil, Chicago

Business: A Practical Journal of the Office, New York and Chicago

Charles Austin Bates Criticisms, New York

The Chautauquan, Chatauqua, N.Y.

The Christian Union, New York

The Graphic Arts, Boston

The Inland Printer, Chicago

Judge, New York

Judicious Advertising, Chicago

The Keystone, PRR Technical and Historical Society

The Modern Poster Annual, New York: A. Broun

The Needle, Los Angeles: Young & McCallister

New York Central Lines Magazine, New York: New York Central Lines

New York Herald Tribune, New York

The New York Visitor, New York: New York Central System

The Outlook, New York

The Overland Monthly, San Francisco

Pacific Coast Advertising, Los Angeles

Pencil Points, New York

The Poster, Chicago

The Poster, London

Printed Salesmanship / The Printing Art, Chicago

Printers' Ink, New York

Printers' Ink Monthly, New York

Profitable Advertising, Boston

Railway Age, Chicago

Santa Fe Magazine, Topeka, Kans.: AT&SF Rwy.

Saturday Night, Los Angeles

Signs of the Times, Cincinnati

Southern Pacific Bulletin, San Francisco: Southern Pacific Co.

Sunset, San Francisco

Town & Country, New York

Western Advertising, San Francisco

Exhibition Catalogs

Art Directors Club of New York, Annual of Advertising Art, 1921–1954

Posters in an Age of Elegance, Chadds Ford, Pa.: Brandywine River Museum, 1999

Family, Corporate, and State Archives

Burlington Northern Santa Fe Corporate Art Collection

Couse Family Archives

Maurer Family Archives

Pennsylvania State Archives

Proceedings of the American Association of General Passenger and Ticket Agents, Sept. 16, 1890, pp. 61–62; Barriger Library, St. Louis Mercantile Library

Sam Hyde Harris Family

Southern Pacific Co. Advertising Files

INDEX

Page numbers in italics refer to illustrations. The abbreviations "RR" and "Ry." refer to "Railroad" and "Railway," respectively.

Advertising Arts, 105
Advertising strategy: backlash against, 22; brand
    identity as, 3–4, 6, 10, 14, 61; comfortable
    travel as, xi, 4, 13, 17–18, 23, 40, 48, 50, 94,
    111, 126; copy as, 3–4, 18, 30, 34; expendi-
    tures on, 22, 27, 52, 104; innovation as, 4, 34;
    lure of place as, xi, 6–9, 15, 22–24, 27, 43, 50,
    52, 55, 61, 81, 83, 111; theory of, 9–10
The Advertising World (British periodical), 22, 47
African Americans, depiction of, 17, *19,* 93
Agnew, W. L., 18–19, 30
Air travel, 81, 132
"Alton Girls," 6
American West. *See specific destinations*
Art Deco movement, 79, 81, 109
Art posters, 1, 9–10, 12, 21, 63–74
Arts and Crafts movement, 17, 76
AT&SF (Atchison, Topeka & Santa Fe Ry.). *See*
    Santa Fe Ry.

Atchison, Topeka & Santa Fe Ry. (AT&SF). *See*
    Santa Fe Ry.
Automobiles, 38–39, 48, 50, 63, 94, 103

Baltimore & Ohio RR, 4, *5,* 50, *81,* 83, *86, 132*
Barns, postering/painting of, 22
Bates, Charles Austin, 12–13, 19
Beebe, Lucius, 104–105
Benton, Harry Stacy, 34
Bernhard, Lucian, 39, 103
Bethers, Ray, 111
Big Four Route, 4, 6, 10, *12,* 26
The Bill Poster (periodical), 12–13, 21
Billboards, 1, 10, 19, 21; animated, 85, *88;*
    automobile travel and, 48, 94; Binner and,
    17–18, 30; Great Northern and, 83;
    Northern Pacific and, 39, *40;* Santa Fe Ry.
    and, 39–41, *41,* 79; wartime advertising and,
    125, *126*

Binder, Joseph, 93, 103
Binner, Oscar, 17–19, 30, 57
Birchfield, Carlton J., 41, 43–44, *46,* 76, 125
Birdseye, Roger, 125
Bishop, Jim, 126–132
Bonestell, Chesley, 68, 74, *75*
Booklets, illustrated, xi, 2, 10, 22, 38, 52, 95
Borough, Randal, 52, *55, 56*
Boyer, S. A., 103
Bradley, Will H., 12, 17
Brand identity, 3–4, 6, 10, 14, 61. *See also* Logos
Brangwyn, Frank, 68
Bremer, Edward P., 83
British advertising, 12, 22, 39, 50, 68
Broadsides, xi, 1–2, 83, 104
Broadway Limited (PRR), 85, 126, *131*
Broders, Roger, 50
Browne, Charles Francis, 21–22
Brubaker, Jon O., 68, *71,* 103

Bryn, Oscar Martinez, 41, 43–46, 50, 74, 109, 126, *129*
Budd Company. *See* Edward G. Budd Company
Bull, William Howell, 15, *16*, 27, *28, 29, 33*, 57, 105
Burbank, E. A., 6
Bureau of Railway Economics, U.S., 50
Burlington RR. *See* Chicago, Burlington & Quincy RR

Calendars, xi, 4; Chesapeake & Ohio RR, 94; Chicago & Alton RR, 6; Great Northern RR, 83; New York Central RR, 63, 67–68, 95; Pennsylvania RR, 85, *88;* Santa Fe Ry., 6, 50, 79; Southern Pacific RR, 27
California, 22–23; New York Central RR, 68, *71;* Rock Island RR, 27, 30, *31;* Santa Fe Ry., 24, 39–41, *41,* 126; Southern Pacific RR, 8, 14–15, 24, 26–27, *55,* 57, *59,* 61
California Limited (AT&SF), 24, 39, *43, 44, 50,* 52, *54*
Calkins, Earnest Elmo, 30, 34, *35,* 68
Campbell, James M., 27, 30, 34
Canadian Pacific Ry., 50, 58, 81, *82, 83*
Car cards, 30, 34–36, *34, 35, 36,* 55, *57,* 63, 85, *89*
Carey, Paul, 46, 58, 61, 111
Cars, railroad, 4, 23, 39, 103, 125–126
Cassandre, A. M., 103, 111
Central Railroad of New Jersey, 36, *105*
Century Publishing Company, 12
Charles Daniel Frey (ad agency), 85
Charlton, James J., 6
Chenoweth, Joseph, 81
Chéret, Jules, 1, 10, 22, 39
Chesapeake & Ohio RR, 8, 94
Chicago, 50, *51,* 74, 85, *86, 87,* 95, *112*
Chicago, Burlington & Quincy RR, 4, 18, 27, 30, 34, 104–105, *106*
Chicago, Milwaukee & St. Paul RR (CM&SP), 4, 6, 13–14, *14,* 18, *19*
Chicago, Rock Island & Pacific RR. *See* Rock Island RR
Chicago & Alton RR, 6, 17
Chicago & North Western RR, 4, 8
Chicago Great Western Ry., 6, 17–18, *18, 19,* 34, *36*
Chicago interurban lines, 50, *86,* 95
The Chief (AT&SF), 74, 76–81, *76, 77, 78, 80*
Circus posters, 1–2, 13
City of San Francisco (SP), 111
CM&SP. *See* Chicago, Milwaukee & St. Paul RR
Colorado, 23, 30, *32*
Colorado Midland Ry., 13
Colton, Wendell P., 34
Commodore Vanderbilt (NYC), 105

Cotsworth, Albert, Jr., 105
Couse, Eanger Irving, 79
Cret, Paul, 104
CRI&P (Chicago, Rock Island & Pacific RR). *See* Rock Island RR
The Crusader (Jersey Central RR), *105*

D'Alesi, Hugo, 22, *23*
Daniels, George Henry, 10, *10,* 22, 67
Daylight (SP), 111
Delaware, Lackawanna & Western RR, 34, *35*
Denslow, William W., 13–14
Denver & Rio Grande RR, 7
Depew, Chauncey, 10, 18
Dewitt Clinton (NYC), 105
Display windows, 23–30, 39, 79, *81*
Dixon, Maynard, 27, 52, 55
Dodge, H. D., 76
Dreyfuss, Henry, 124

Edward G. Budd Company, 85, 126
Eggleston, Edward, 88
Elam, L. Vasser, 83, *86*
Empire State Express (NYC), 10, *11,* 67, *123,* 124
Ethridge, George, 30, 67
European advertising, xi, 1, 12, 22, 30, 38–39, 50, 93

Fancher, Louis, 48, *49*
Fayant, Frank H., 67
Fee, Chas. S., 8, 20n12, 26, 30
Finn, Joseph H., 105
First Santa Fe Train (lithograph), 24–26, *25, 26*
Forbes Lithographic Company, 30, *31, 32*
Formats, poster: eight sheet, 17, 30; forty-eight sheet, 18; large, 3, 8, 24, 30; quarter sheet, 52, 61; single sheet, 1, 39, 48, 85; twenty-four sheet, 39, 48
Foster, William Harnden, 67
Fraser, Ivor, 48
French advertising, 1, 22, 40, 50

Geary, Fred, 76
General Motors, 126
Georgi, Edwin, 125, *126*
German advertising, 13, 39–40, 58
Golden State Limited (CRI&P), 27, 30, *31*
Goodsill, Max, 83
Grand Canyon, 8–9, 24, 43, 50, *51,* 126, *129*
Great Northern RR, 30, 83
Great Western Ry. (Britain), 39, *40*
Greene, Walter, 68, *74*
Gull, Ivar, 85, *89*
Gutekunst, Frederick, 8

Halftone technology, xi, 3, 21
Hall, Haines, 111, *112*
Hansen, Anthony, 68
Hanson, Oscar Rabe, *86,* 95
Harper's (periodical), 12, 14, 18, 93
Harris, Sam Hyde, 50–52, *50, 51, 52, 53, 54,* 55, *55*
Haynes, F. Jay, 8
Hazell, Frank, 68, *74*
Held, John, Jr., 63, *65, 66,* 97
Higgins, Charles A., 26, 79
Hill, Bern, 126, *131*
Hilton, J., 83
Hohlwein, Ludwig, 13, 43
Hollingsworth, Will, 81, *83*
Horter, Earl, 68, *73*
Hotel Del Monte, 7, 9, 55
Hudson River RR. *See* New York Central RR
Hunter, W. B., 34

IC. *See* Illinois Central RR
Illian, George, 83
Illinois Central RR (IC), 34, 50, 83–85, *86, 87*
Ingalls, George H., 67
Ingram, K. C., 50, 61, 76
The Inland Printer (periodical), 39, 43
Ives, Frederick, 3

Jackson, William H., 8, 10
The Jeffersonian (PRR), 114, *119*

Keith, William, 81
Kelly, James, 109
Kihn, W. Langdon, 81, *82*
Krollmann, Gustav, 83, *84*

Lackawanna RR, 34, *35*
Lake Shore & Michigan Southern RR, 17, *17*
"Lake Shore girls," 17, *17*
Lake Shore Railroads, 2, *2*
Langtry, Lillie, 6
Larned, W. Livingston, 132
Laurence, Sydney M., 83, *85*
Lee, Ivy, 85, 88
Lehigh Valley RR, 6
Lenz, Alfred, 81
Lerner, George, 125, *126*
Leyendecker, J. C., 12, 22, 81
"Limited" trains, xi, 3, 18. *See also specific trains*
Lithographs, landscape, 8–9
LNER. *See* London & North Eastern Ry.
Lockwood, P. V. D., 74
Loewy, Raymond, 114, 124
Logan, Maurice, 46, 52, 55, 57–58, *58, 59, 60,* 61–63, *61, 62, 63, 64,* 111

Logos, 4, *5,* 13, 17, 46–47, 76, 79, *94,* 105. *See also*
 Brand identity
London & North Eastern Ry. (LNER), 50, 68
London Midland & Scotland Ry., 50
London Underground, 39
Lord, Daniel M., 4
Lord & Thomas (ad agency), 4, 57. *See also* Lord
 & Thomas and Logan
Lord & Thomas and Logan (ad agency), 68,
 92n14. *See also* Lord & Thomas
Louisville, New Albany & Chicago Ry., 6, 26
Ludekens, Fred, 46, 61, 111
Lummis, Charles F., 81

Madan, Fredrick, 68
Magazines, 3, 10, 12, 22, 30, 38, 93, 126
Maps, 4, 6, *6, 7,* 13, *13,* 24
Margolin, Victor, 21
Markham, Charles H., 85
Markland, John, 93–94
Maurer, Sascha, xi, 97, 103, *103, 104,* 111–124,
 114, 115, 116, 117, 118, 119, 126–132
McCormick, Edward O., 4, 6, 10, 26–27
Mead, George, 18
Megargee, Lon, 76
Michigan Central RR, 8
Mizen, Fred, 109
Modernism, 93, 95, 104
Monon Route (Louisville, New Albany & Chicago
 Ry.), 6, *6,* 26
Moran, Thomas, 8, 24, 83
Morse, Metcalf, 55
M-10000 and M-10001 (UP), 103–104, 105

Nason, Ben, 126
Native Americans, depiction of, xi, *122;* on
 calendars, 6; by Canadian Pacific RR, 81, *82;*
 by Colorado Midland RR, 13; on magazine
 covers, 27, 52; by Northern Pacific RR, 83,
 85; by Santa Fe Ry., 24, 43, *44, 54,* 76–81, *76,*
 77, 78, 79, 80, 125, *128*
The Needle *(periodical),* 44
New England, 63, *65, 66, 116, 117,* 126
New Haven RR. *See* New York, New Haven &
 Hartford RR
New Jersey Central RR, 36, *105*
New York, 68, *72, 73, 75, 89,* 97, *99, 100, 101, 102*
New York, New Haven & Hartford RR, 50, 63, *65,*
 66, 97, 103, *103,* 111–114, *114, 115, 116, 117,*
 125, 126, *126*
New York & Chicago Limited (PRR), 4, *5*
New York Art Directors Club, 68, 83, 111, 114
New York Central RR (NYC), 38, 50, 63, 67–74,
 65, 66, 67, 69, 70, 71, 72, 73, 74, 75, 94–97,

95, 96, 97, 98, 99, 100, 101, 102; booklets of,
 95; calendars of, 63, 67–68, 95; destination
 advertising and, 10, 13, 63, 68, *71,* 94, 126,
 126, 127; streamliners and, 105, *108, 121, 123,*
 124; ticket offices of, 23–24; wartime advertising and, 125, *126. See also specific trains*
Newspapers, 2, 22, 104
Niagara Falls, 7–8, 13, *99*
Norris, James, 1
North Coast Limited (NP), 81, 83
Northern Pacific RR (NP), 8, 39, *40,* 50, 81, 83,
 84, 85

Object posters *(Sachplakate),* 39
Olmstead, Frederick Law, Jr., 22
Oriental Limited (Great Northern RR), 83
Overland Limited (SP), 27, *29,* 61, *62*

Panama Pacific Exposition (1915), 38, 44
Paris Lyons Méditerranée Ry. (France), 22, *23,* 50
Parrish, Maxfield, 12, 94
Patterson, Russell, 68
Pencil Points (periodical), 97
Penfield, Edward, 12
Pennsylvania Limited (PRR), 4
Pennsylvania Railroad ("Pennsy," PRR), 50, 126;
 calendars of, 85, *88;* destination advertising
 and, 23, 85, *89, 90, 91,* 109, *111, 119,* 126;
 landscape photographs and, 8; "limiteds"
 and, 3, *130;* logo of, 4, *5;* patriotic advertising
 and, 85–88, *90, 91,* 114, *119;* streamliners
 and, 109, *111,* 114, *120,* 124; women in
 posters of, 13, 114, *119. See also specific*
 trains
Philadelphia & Reading RR, 34
Phoebe Snow car cards, 34, *35*
Photographs, 8, 10, 18, 24, 38
Pick, Frank, 39
The Pioneer Limited (CM&SP), 18, *19*
The Poster (periodical), 39, 43
Powers, Lyman, 125, *126*
Pratt, Edwin A., 24
Presbrey, Frank, 1, 23–24, 30, 39
Printers' Ink (periodical), 22, 30
Procter & Gamble Company, 30, 93
Proehl, Paul, 85, *87*
Pullman Company, 105, 109, 124
Pyle, Howard, 94

Rackow, Leo, 105, *109*
Radio advertising, 104
Ragan, Leslie, 74, 94–97, *94, 95, 96, 97, 98, 99,*
 100, 101, 102, 121, 122, 123, 124, 125–126,
 126, 127

Railroads: automobiles and, 38–39, 48, 50, 63, 94,
 103; competition among, 2–6, 12, 17–18, 22–
 23; hotels built by, 7, 9, 55; regulation of, 38,
 47; transcontinental routes of, 2, 7, 15, 81.
 See also specific railroads and trains
Railway Age (periodical), 50, 83
Rau, William, 8
Rea, Samuel, 85
Reed, Ethel, 13–14
Rehag, Morris, 111
Reid, Robert O., 68
Reiss, Winold, 83
Remington, Frederic, 22
Rhead, Louis, 12
Rinehart, F. A., 6
Rock Island RR (CRI&P), 6, 27, 30, *31, 32*
Rowell, John, 22
Russell, C. Philip, 50

St. Paul. *See* Chicago, Milwaukee & St. Paul
Santa Fe de-Luxe (AT&SF), 39–43, *41, 42, 44*
Santa Fe Ry. (AT&SF), 39–47, 50–52, 74, 76–81;
 advertising strategy of, 76; billboards and,
 39–40, *41,* 79; calendars of, 6, 50, 79; com-
 fortable travel and, 40; destination advertis-
 ing and, 8, 24, 39, *41, 42, 43, 44, 45,* 125–126,
 128, 129; German design and, 39–40; logo of,
 46–47, 76, 79. *See also specific trains*
Sauerwein, Frank P., 24–26, *25*
Seaboard Air-Line Ry., *33*
"See America First" movement, 24, 30
The Seminole (Illinois Central RR), 85
Shepard, Otis, 103
Show posters. *See* Circus posters
Simpson, William H., 24, 26, 39–40, 43, 46, 79, 125
Snow trains, 97, 103. *See also* Winter sports
South Pacific Coast Ry., 3–4, *4*
The South Wind (PRR), 114, *120,* 124
Southern Pacific RR (SP), *33,* 50, 52–61, *55, 56,*
 57, 58, 59, 60, 61, 62, 63, 64; archive of,
 destroyed, 30; billboards and, 52, 94; brand
 identity and, 8, 14, 61; calendars of, 27;
 comfort advertising and, 94, 111; destination
 advertising and, 7–8, *9,* 14–15, *15, 16,* 24, 26–
 27, *29,* 30, 52, *55,* 57, *59,* 61, 111; display
 windows and, 24; photographs and, 8;
 streamliners and, 109, 111, *112, 113;* wartime
 advertising and, 48, *49, 126. See also specific*
 trains
Sperr, Perry L., 97
Stebbins, Hal, 47, 61
Stewart, J. N., 39
Stokes, C. W., 81
Stoops, Herbert Morton, 68, *69, 70*

Streamline trains, xi, 103–124, *105, 106, 107, 108, 112, 113, 114, 115, 116, 117, 121, 123*
Strobridge, Nelson, 2
Stubbs, John Christian, 15, *15*
Sunset (periodical), 15, 27, *27, 28,* 52
Sunset Limited (SP), 14–15, *15, 16,* 52, *55,* 57, 81, 105
Super Chief (AT&SF), 125

Teague, Walter D., 103
Teasdale, William, 50, 67
Technological innovations, 1, 4, 34, 38, 125
Teller, Grif, 88, 109, *111*
Thomas F. Logan, Inc. (ad agency), 67, 92n14. *See also* Lord & Thomas and Logan
Ticket offices, 23–24, 39, 52
Timetables, xi, 2, 4, 34, 85
Tipple, Fred, 126
Titus, Hazen J., 39
Trademarks. *See* Logos
Transcontinental & Western Airlines, 81
Transcontinental routes, 2, 7, 15, 81, 109
"Travel by Train" campaign, 63, 103, 109

Tredway, F. Q., 109
Treidler, Adolph, 68, *72,* 103
Treviso, Louis, 39–47, *42, 43, 44, 46, 47,* 50, 63, 74, 111
Twain, Mark, 34
20th Century Limited (NYC), *24,* 39, 67, 105, *121,* 124
Typography, 39, 41, 61, 97

Union Pacific RR (UP), 2, *3, 29,* 103–105, *107,* 109, 126

Veenstra, H. M., 109
Villa, Hernando G., 74–81, *76, 77, 78, 79, 80, 81*

Wabash RR, 6
Warner, Charles Dudley, 14
Wartime advertising, 47, 48, *49,* 125
Watkins, Carleton E., 8
Watson, Ernest W., 126
Weill, Alain, 1, 93
Weinhardt, Carl J., 50, 63

Welsh, William P., 109, *110*
Wenrich, John, 97
Werntz, Carl Newland, 46, 94
West, American. *See specific destinations*
Western Advertising (periodical), 47, 58, 63, 111
Wheeler, Olin Dunbar, 81, 83
Wilkinson, Norman, 50, 68
Willmarth, William, 105, 126, *130*
Winter sports, 55, 97, 103, 126
Women, depiction of, xi, 6, 13, *13,* 17, *17, 18,* 39, 43, 58, *59, 60, 61,* 63, *65, 66,* 68, 76, 109, *109, 110*
"Wonderland." *See* Yellowstone National Park
Woodcuts, 1, 12
Woolett, Prudence, 76
Wyeth, N. C., 85, 88, *90, 91,* 94

Yellowstone National Park, 7, 81, 83
Yosemite National Park, 8, 26, *60,* 61, *63*

Zephyr (Chicago, Burlington & Quincy RR), 104–105, *106*

For the past decade MICHAEL E. ZEGA has researched and written about railroad advertising and promotion, visiting collections as diverse as the Huntington Library, the Couse Family Archives, and Smithsonian's Ethnology Archives. He has contributed articles to *Vintage Rails* and *Classic Trains* magazines. His latest work, in the *Journal of the Southwest,* "Advertising the Southwest," traces the beginnings of the Santa Fe's famous promotional campaign.

JOHN E. GRUBER is president of the Center for Railroad Photography and Art (www.railphoto-art.org) and editor of its magazine, *Railroad Heritage.* A freelance railroad photographer, he received a railroad history award from the Railway & Locomotive Historical Society in 1994 for lifetime achievement in photography, and appeared on the *Tracks Ahead* television program (volume six, 1995). He is contributing editor to *Classic Trains,* preservation columnist for *Trains,* and co-author of *Caboose* (2001). He was editor of *Vintage Rails* magazine from 1995 to 1999.

BOOK AND JACKET DESIGNER sharon sklar
COPYEDITOR miki bird
COMPOSITOR sharon sklar
TYPEFACES minion and frutiger
BOOK AND JACKET PRINTER four colour imports

ROUTES OF THE RAILROADS

A BALTIMORE & OHIO

B CANADIAN PACIFIC

C CENTRAL OF NEW JERSEY

D CHICAGO & ALTON

E CHICAGO, BURLINGTON & QUINCY

F CHICAGO GREAT WESTERN

G CHICAGO, MILWAUKEE & ST. PAUL

H DELAWARE, LACKAWANNA & WESTERN

I ILLINOIS CENTRAL

J MONON

K NEW YORK CENTRAL

L NEW HAVEN

M NORTHERN PACIFIC

N PENNSYLVANIA RAILROAD

O SANTA FE

P SEABOARD AIR LINE

Q SOUTHERN PACIFIC

R UNION PACIFIC